McGraw-Hill's

500 MCAT
Organic Chemistry
Questions

to know by test day

Also in McGraw-Hill's 500 Questions Series

McGraw-Hill's
500 MCAT
Organic Chemistry
Questions
to know by test day

John T. Moore, EdD, and Richard H. Langley, PhD

New York   Chicago   San Francisco   Lisbon   London   Madrid   Mexico City
Milan   New Delhi   San Juan   Seoul   Singapore   Sydney   Toronto

The **McGraw·Hill** Companies

John Moore, EdD, has taught chemistry at Stephen F. Austin State University for more than 40 years, where he is the Director of the Teaching Excellence Center and Codirector of the Science, Technology, Engineering and Mathematics Center.

Richard H. Langley, PhD, has taught chemistry at the university level for more than 30 years and has coauthored numerous books on the subject. He has written questions for the AP Chemistry exam and taught General Chemistry and Organic Chemistry MCAT review courses.

1 2 3 4 5 6 7 8 9 10 11 12 13 14 15 16 16 17   QFR/QFR   1 9 8 7 6 5 4 3 2

ISBN   978-0-07-178275-3
MHID   0-07-178275-3

e-ISBN   978-0-07-178276-0
e-MHID   0-07-178276-1

Library of Congress Control Number 2011944613

Illustrations by Cenveo

MCAT is a registered trademark of the Association of American Medical Colleges, which was not involved in the production of, and does not endorse, this product.

McGraw-Hill products are available at special quantity discounts to use as premiums and sales promotions or for use in corporate training programs. To contact a representative, please e-mail us at bulksales@mcgraw-hill.com.

This book is printed on acid-free paper.

CONTENTS

INTRODUCTION

Congratulations! You've taken a big step toward MCAT success by purchasing *McGraw-Hill's 500 MCAT Organic Chemistry Questions to Know by Test Day*. We are here to help you take the next step and score high on your MCAT exam so you can get into the medical school of your choice!

This book gives you 500 MCAT-style multiple-choice questions that cover all the most essential course material. Each question is clearly explained in the answer key. The questions will give you valuable independent practice to supplement your regular textbook and the ground you have already covered in your organic chemistry class.

This book and the others in the series were written by expert chemistry teachers who know the MCAT inside and out and can identify crucial information as well as the kinds of questions that are most likely to appear on the exam.

You might be the kind of student who needs to study extra a few weeks before the exam for a final review. Or you might be the kind of student who puts off preparing until the last minute before the exam. No matter what your preparation style, you will benefit from reviewing these 500 questions, which closely parallel the content, format, and degree of difficulty of the questions on the actual MCAT exam. These questions and the explanations in the answer key are the ideal last-minute study tool for those final weeks before the test.

If you practice with all the questions and answers in this book, we are certain you will build the skills and confidence needed to excel on the MCAT. Good luck!

—*Editors of McGraw-Hill Education*

CHAPTER 1

The Fundamentals

1. The following illustration is a section of a carbon nanotube.

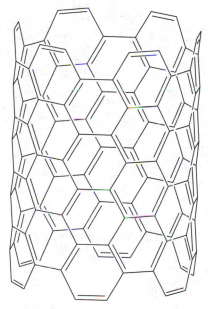

What is the best description of the hybridization of the carbon atoms?

(A) sp^3 only
(B) sp^2 only
(C) sp^2 and sp^3
(D) sp and sp^2

2. Which of the following is the best resonance structure for HOCN?

(A) $H—\ddot{\overset{..}{O}}—C\equiv N:$

(B) $H—\overset{\oplus}{\underset{..}{O}}=C=\overset{\ominus}{\underset{..}{N}}:$

(C) $H—\ddot{O}=C\equiv N:$

(D) $H—\ddot{\underset{..}{O}}\overset{\ominus}{}—\overset{\oplus}{\underset{..}{C}}=N:$

3. Which of the following are reasonable resonance structures for nitrobenzene?

I   II   III

(A) I, II, and III
(B) I and III
(C) II and III
(D) I and II

4. Choose the strongest acid from the following.

(A)

(B)

(C)

(D)

5. What is the hybridization of the nitrogen atoms in the following compound?

$$\overset{\oplus}{N}=N:$$

(A) Both are sp³ hybridized.
(B) Both are sp hybridized.
(C) One is sp hybridized, and the other is sp³ hybridized.
(D) One is sp hybridized, and the other is sp² hybridized.

6. Why is ortho-nitrophenol a stronger acid than phenol?

(A) destabilization of the aromatic system
(B) electron donation by the nitro group
(C) steric crowding between the –OH and the –NO₂
(D) resonance stabilization of the anion

7. What are the hybridizations of the indicated atoms?

(A) 1 = sp², 2 = sp², and 3 = sp²
(B) 1 = sp, 2 = sp, and 3 = sp²
(C) 1 = sp³, 2 = sp³, and 3 = sp²
(D) 1 = sp, 2 = sp³, and 3 = sp²

8. Which of the following is NOT a disubstituted cyclohexane?

(A)

(B)

(C)

(D)

9. The C-C bonds in 1,3-butadiene utilize which of the following types of orbitals?
   (A) sp^3 orbitals
   (B) sp orbitals
   (C) sp^2 orbitals
   (D) unhybridized s orbitals

10. The compounds cis-1,2-dibromopropene and trans-1,2-dibromopropene are examples of
    (A) structural isomers
    (B) conformers
    (C) diastereomers
    (D) geometric isomers

11. Why is the triflate group a better leaving group than a hydroxyl group? The structure of the triflate group is

    (A) It stabilizes carbocations.
    (B) It is stabilized by resonance.
    (C) It is a stronger base.
    (D) It is a good fluoride donor.

12. The compound 1,3,5-hexatriene contains a conjugated system. The bond between C(4) and C(5) is shorter than a normal alkane C-C bond. The reason for this behavior is that the bond formed between two sp^2 hybridized atoms

    (A) has less s-character
    (B) has more s-character
    (C) has more p-character
    (D) is lower energy

13. The carbonyl group has a carbon-oxygen double bond. The double bond consists of one σ bond and one π bond. The carbon atom is sp^2 hybridized. Therefore, the carbon has

    (A) an unhybridized p-orbital and three equivalent orbitals
    (B) an unhybridized p-orbital and two equivalent orbitals
    (C) two unhybridized p-orbital and two equivalent orbitals
    (D) four equivalent hybridized orbitals

14. It is possible to use an acid to catalyze the hydrolysis of an ester. The acid is considered a catalyst because it

    (A) is possible to use any amount
    (B) alters the heat of reaction
    (C) stabilizes the intermediate
    (D) reacts in a one-to-one ratio with the ester

15. In the following ion, rank the indicated bonds from longest to shortest.

(A) 3 > 1 = 2
(B) 1 > 3 = 2
(C) 3 = 2 > 1
(D) 1 = 2 > 3

16. Which of the indicated hydrogen atoms in the following compound is the most acidic?

(A) 3
(B) 1
(C) 2
(D) 4

17. The following molecule contains both σ and π bonds. How many π bonds are present?

(A) 9
(B) 10
(C) 8
(D) 7

18. The following molecule does NOT contain which of the following functional groups?

(A) amide
(B) nitrile
(C) amine
(D) phosphate

19. What is the IUPAC name for the following compound?

    (A) 5-hexyn-3-ol
    (B) 1-hexyn-4-ol
    (C) cis-5-hexyn-3-ol
    (D) 4-hydroxy-1-hexyne

20. What is the IUPAC name for the following compound?

    (A) 4-hydroxy-1-isopropyl-2-hepten-1-one
    (B) 2-hydroxy-6-methyl-3-hepten-5-one
    (C) 6-hydroxy-2-methyl-4-hepten-3-al
    (D) 6-hydroxy-2-methyl-4-hepten-3-one

21. How many σ bonds and π bonds are in benzene?
    (A) 6 σ and 3 π
    (B) 12 σ and 3 π
    (C) 12 σ and 6 π
    (D) 6 σ and 6 π

22. During the complete hydrogenation of one mole of $C_{10}H_{14}$, two moles of hydrogen were absorbed. How many rings were present in the original compound?
    (A) 2
    (B) 1
    (C) 3
    (D) 5

23. A compound with the general formula $C_{10}H_{14}O$ could NOT contain which of the following functional groups?
    (A) ether
    (B) alcohol
    (C) acid anhydride
    (D) alkene

24. Which of the following series best relates the order of increasing C-N bond length?

    (A) $CH_3NH_2 < CN^- < OCN^-$
    (B) $CH_3NH_2 < OCN^- < CN^-$
    (C) $CN^- < CH_3NH_2 < OCN^-$
    (D) $CN^- < OCN^- < CH_3NH_2$

25. The conformation of two groups about the central carbon-carbon bond, which is most stable, is

    (A) eclipsed
    (B) anti
    (C) gauche
    (D) cis

26. What is the IUPAC name for the following compound?

$$CH_3-CH_2-CH_2 \quad\quad CH_2-CH_3$$
$$C=C$$
$$H \quad\quad H$$

    (A) (Z)-4-heptene
    (B) (Z)-3-heptene
    (C) (E)-3-heptene
    (D) (E)-4-heptene

27. What is the name of the following compound?

    (A) 2,4,5-methylheptane
    (B) 3,4,6-trimethylheptane
    (C) isodecane
    (D) 2,4,5-trimethylheptane

28. What is the name of the following compound?

(A) 3-bromo-4-chlorohexane
(B) trans-3-bromo-4-chlorohexane
(C) E-3-bromo-4-chlorohexane
(D) 1-bromo-2-chloro-1,2-diethylethane

29. Which of the following is an acid anhydride?

(A)

(B)

(C)

(D)

30. How many isomers of hexane are there?
(A) 7
(B) 6
(C) 5
(D) 4

31. Which of the following is an isobutyl group?

(A)

CH_3—CH_2—CH_2—CH_2—

(B)

CH_3—$C(CH_3)(CH_3)$—CH_3

(C) CH_3—CH_2—CH(CH_3)—

(D)

CH_3—$CH(CH_3)$—CH_2—

32. What is the IUPAC name for the drug Tylenol shown as follows?

(A) N-(4-hydroxyphenyl)acetamide
(B) 4-(N-aceto)phenol
(C) N-(4-phenol)-N-acetoamine
(D) N-(p-phenol)acetamide

33. What is the IUPAC name for the following compound?

(A) 2-fluoro-5-nonanone
(B) propyl 4-fluoropentanoate
(C) 4-fluoropentyl propyl ether
(D) 4-fluoropentyl propanoate

34. Which of the following compounds has four degrees of unsaturation?

(A)

(B)

(C)

(D)

35. Two cysteine molecules in a protein may undergo oxidation to form a disulfide linkage. It is possible to reverse this process by adding a suitable reducing agent. The process is

What is the change in the oxidation state of the sulfur atoms during reduction?

(A) 1 to −2
(B) 2 to −1
(C) 2 to 0
(D) 1 to 0

36. What is the name of the following compound?

- (A) 4-bromo-6-hydroxy-3-methylheptane
- (B) 4-bromo-3-methyl-heptan-6-ol
- (C) 4-bromo-2-hydroxy-5-methylheptane
- (D) 4-bromo-5-methyl-heptan-2-ol

37. Which of the following is an acetal?

(A)

(B)

(C)

(D)

38. What is the IUPAC name for the following compound?

(A) (E)-6-octenoic acid
(B) (Z)-2-octenoic acid
(C) (E)-2-octenoic acid
(D) (Z)-6-octenoic acid

39. How many different isomeric compounds with the formula C_9H_{18} will yield 3-isopropylhexane upon catalytic hydrogenation?

(A) 10
(B) 7
(C) 11
(D) 8

40. Distillation of crude oil yields many compounds. One of the compounds is $C_{14}H_{14}$. What is the degree of unsaturation of this compound?

(A) 12
(B) 6
(C) 10
(D) 8

41. The compound C_3H_5Br could be any of the following EXCEPT

(A) trans-2-bromopropene
(B) bromocyclopropane
(C) trans-1-bromopropene
(D) cis-1-bromopropene

42. Which of the isomers of ethylcyclohexane is the most stable?

(A) axial
(B) equatorial
(C) cis
(D) trans

43. The free radical monochlorination of 2-methylbutane will give the following products.

What is the relationship between these products?

(A) stereoisomers
(B) conformers
(C) structural isomers
(D) diastereomers

44. The structure of the drug Demerol is:

How many sp^3 hybridized carbon atoms are present in Demerol?

(A) 4
(B) 5
(C) 6
(D) 8

45. Which of the following is the most stable hydrocarbon?

(A)

(B)

(C)

(D)

46. What is the hybridization on each of the indicated nitrogen atoms?

(A) I is sp, II is sp³, and III is sp²
(B) I is sp, II is sp², and III is sp
(C) I is p, II is sp², and III is sp²
(D) I is sp³, II is sp², and III is sp²

47. Rank the following acids from strongest to weakest.

I

II

III

H-Cl

IV

(A) IV > II > I > III
(B) III > I > II > IV
(C) IV > II > III > I
(D) II > I > III > IV

48. What are the approximate values of each of the indicated bond angles in the structure of the amino acid histidine?

(A) 1 = 109.5° and 2 = 109.5°
(B) 1 = 90° and 2 = 120°
(C) 1 = 120° and 2 = 109.5°
(D) 1 = 109.5° and 2 = 120°

49. Which orbitals interact when CH_3^+ reacts with CH_3^- to form CH_3CH_3?

(A) p and sp^3
(B) sp^2 and sp^2
(C) sp^3 and sp^3
(D) s and p

50. The following compounds are examples of

(A) enantiomers
(B) conformers
(C) regioisomers
(D) diastereomers

51. The compound 1,3,5-hexatriene contains a conjugated system. All the C-C single bonds are shorter than normal C-C single bonds. The reason for this shortening is that there is
(A) double-bond character due to resonating σ-electrons
(B) partial overlap of the unhybridized p-orbitals on the two carbon atoms
(C) an interaction between the sp^2 and sp^3 hybridized orbitals on the two carbon atoms
(D) bond shortening when two sp^3 hybridized orbitals overlap

52. The compound 3-hexene exists as cis and trans isomers. Which has the greater heat of hydrogenation?
(A) Both isomers are the same.
(B) The trans isomer has the greater heat of hydrogenation.
(C) The cis isomer has the greater heat of hydrogenation.
(D) It is impossible to tell from the data in the problem.

53. Determine the degree of unsaturation in $C_6H_{10}O_4$.
(A) 2
(B) 1
(C) 3
(D) 4

CHAPTER 2

Isomers and Physical Properties

54. Resonance stabilizes many compounds. The following is an example of resonance.

Which of these compounds would benefit the most from this type of resonance?

(A) amide
(B) ester
(C) carboxylic acid
(D) acid chloride

55. Which of the following is (1R,3S)-1,3-dibromo-1,3-difluorobutane?

(A)

(B)

(C)

(D)

56. What is the relationship between the following two compounds?

   (A) identical
   (B) enantiomers
   (C) diastereomers
   (D) conformers

57. Which of the following compounds is NOT polar?

   (A)

   (B)

   (C)

   (D)

58. Compounds I and II are enantiomers. Which of the following is true concerning these two compounds?

   (A) The two compounds have the same melting point and solubility in ethanol.
   (B) Each is superimposable upon its mirror image.
   (C) They can be interconverted without breaking any bonds.
   (D) They rotate plane-polarized light in the same direction.

59. What is the stereochemistry of the following cyclopropane?

(A) 1S, 2R
(B) 2R, 3S
(C) 1S, 2S
(D) 2S, 3S

60. Why is the following compound achiral (does not exhibit optical activity)?

(A) The Me and Et groups are too similar.
(B) The compound is meso.
(C) The central atom is N not C.
(D) The nitrogen undergoes inversion.

61. What is the maximum number of stereoisomers that could be isolated from the reaction of one racemic mixture with another racemic mixture?

(A) 6
(B) 2
(C) 4
(D) 8

62. The S stereoisomer of a compound reacts with a racemic mixture of another compound. This results in two compounds that are easily separated from the reaction mixture. These two compounds are

(A) tautomers
(B) enantiomers
(C) conformers
(D) diastereomers

63. The following compound has two chiral carbons. What are their absolute configurations?

(A) 2R, 3R
(B) 2R, 3S
(C) 2S, 3S
(D) 2S, 3R

64. Which of the following compounds have a nonzero net dipole moment?

I   II   III

(A) I only
(B) III only
(C) II and III
(D) I and III

65. Arrange the following compounds in order of increasing dipole moment.

I   II   III

(A) I < II < III
(B) III < II < I
(C) I < III < II
(D) III < I < II

66. Which of the following compounds is expected to be the most soluble in water?

(A) HO⌒⌒⌒OH

(B) ⌒⌒⌒

(C) H₂N⌒⌒⌒NH₂

(D) Cl⌒⌒⌒Cl

67. Which of the following is capable of hydrogen bonding to water?

I ⌒⌒⌒OH

II ⌒⌒C(=O)⌒

III ⌒⌒⌒

IV ⌒⌒⌒Cl

(A) IV only
(B) III and IV
(C) I only
(D) I and II

68. Which of the following has an S stereocenter?

(A)

(B)

(C)

(D)

69. Which of the following is an enantiomer of this compound?

(A)

(B)

(C)

(D)

70. Which of the following is NOT a meso compound?

(A)

(B)

(C)

(D)

71. Which of the following compounds is achiral?

I   II   III

(A) III
(B) II
(C) I
(D) I and III

72. Which of the following has an (R) stereocenter?

    I   II   III   IV

    (A) I
    (B) III
    (C) II
    (D) IV

73. Which of the following molecules is polar?
    (A) E-2-pentene
    (B) Z-2-pentene
    (C) 2,3-dimethyl-2-butene
    (D) tetrafluoroethene

74. Which of the following compounds is expected to be the most soluble in water?
    (A) [structure: CH₃CH₂CH₂CH₂OH] OH

    (B) Na_2SO_4

    (C) H_2N [structure] NH_2

    (D) [structure: carboxylic acid] OH

75. What is the best explanation of why compound I has a higher boiling point than compound II?

I   II

(A) Compound II is unstable.
(B) Compound II is nonpolar.
(C) Compound I can ionize.
(D) Compound I has hydrogen bonding.

76. What is the relationship between the following two molecules?

(A) diastereomers
(B) enantiomers
(C) conformers
(D) identical

77. What is the relationship between the following two molecules?

CHO   CHO
H₂N——H   H——NH₂
CH₂OH   CH₂OH

(A) regioisomers
(B) diastereomers
(C) enantiomers
(D) identical

78. The following is one of the nucleotides occurring in DNA. What is the hybridization on the two nitrogen atoms indicated in the drawing?

(A) N1 = sp^3 and N2 = sp^2
(B) N1 = sp^2 and N2 = sp^2
(C) N1 = sp^3 and N2 = sp^3
(D) N1 = sp^2 and N2 = sp

79. The following is a portion of DNA. How many stereoisomers of the molecule are possible?

(A) 8
(B) 4
(C) 2
(D) 16

80. The following molecule is chiral as is the corresponding fluorine derivative. How does the optical rotation of this compound compare to the corresponding fluorine derivative?

(A) One is (+) and one is (–).
(B) Both are (+).
(C) Both are (–).
(D) It is impossible to determine.

81. Tartaric acid exists in several stereoisomeric forms. One of these forms is

What are the absolute configurations of carbon atoms 1 and 2?

(A) Carbon 1 = S, and Carbon 2 = S
(B) Carbon 1 = R, and Carbon 2 = S
(C) Carbon 1 = R, and Carbon 2 = R
(D) Carbon 1 = S, and Carbon 2 = R

82. How many stereoisomers are there for the amino acid isoleucine? The structure of isoleucine is

(A) 3
(B) 4
(C) 2
(D) 8

83. The following compound has a specific rotation of +12°.

What would be the specific rotation of the compound formed by replacing one of the hydrogen atoms with a fluorine atom?

(A) impossible to determine from the information given
(B) +12°
(C) −12°
(D) +19°

84. What are the absolute configurations (from left to right) for the chiral centers in the following molecule?

(A) R, R, S
(B) S, S, R
(C) R, R, R
(D) S, S, S

85. How are the following two molecules related?

(A) They are structural isomers.
(B) They are enantiomers.
(C) They are diastereomers.
(D) They are the same.

86. The structure of aspartame is:

What is the absolute configuration of the indicated carbon in the aspartame?
(A) The carbon is achiral.
(B) The carbon is R.
(C) The carbon is S.
(D) The carbon is meso.

87. What is the relationship between the following two molecules?

(A) They are identical.
(B) They are enantiomers.
(C) They are diastereomers.
(D) They are structural isomers.

88. The compound 3-hexene exists as cis and trans isomers. Which isomer is more stable?
(A) The trans isomer is more stable because trans isomers are more reactive.
(B) The cis isomer is more stable because there is less steric hindrance.
(C) The cis isomer is more stable because it has a chiral center.
(D) The trans isomer is more stable because there is less steric hindrance.

89. The compound 3-hexene exists as cis and trans isomers. Is it easy to convert one isomer to the other?
(A) No, because the conversion would require the breaking of a π bond.
(B) No, because the conversion would require the breaking of a σ bond.
(C) Yes, because the conversion would require the breaking of a weak π bond.
(D) Yes, because the conversion would require the breaking of a weak σ bond.

90. The compound 1,3,5-hexatriene undergoes catalytic hydrogenation. How many moles of hydrogen gas are necessary to completely hydrogenate two moles of 1,3,5-hexatriene?
(A) 12
(B) 3
(C) 6
(D) 9

91. The amino acid alanine, like most amino acids, is chiral. The natural chiral amino acids are the L enantiomers. The synthesis of alanine produces a mixture that contains equal amounts of the D and L enantiomers. The mixture is
    (A) an optically active mixture
    (B) a diastereomeric mixture
    (C) a mesomeric mixture
    (D) a racemic mixture

92. How many stereocenters may a meso compound contain?
    (A) 0
    (B) 1
    (C) 2
    (D) 3

93. An optically active compound that rotates plane-polarized light counter-clockwise is said to be:
    (A) levorotatory
    (B) dextrorotatory
    (C) (R)
    (D) (S)

94. The optically active compound (S)-2-methyl-1-butanol has an optical rotation of $[\alpha]_D^{25} -5.8°$. What is the optical rotation of an equimolar mixture of (S)-2-methyl-1-butanol and (R)-2-methyl-1-butanol?
    (A) +5.8°
    (B) −5.8°
    (C) 0°
    (D) 2 (−5.8°)

95. The compound 2,3-dibromopentane has how many chiral centers?
    (A) 1
    (B) 2
    (C) 0
    (D) 3

96. Compounds A and B are enantiomeric alcohols. If compound A melts at 92°C, what is the melting point of compound B?
    (A) 92°C
    (B) < 92°C
    (C) > 92°C
    (D) impossible to determine

97. A chiral compound with an optical rotation of +12.6° undergoes an S_N2 reaction at the chiral center. The optical rotation of the product would be

(A) impossible to determine
(B) +12.6°
(C) –12.6°
(D) 0°

98. The optical rotation of a certain carboxylic acid is negative, while the optical rotation of its sodium salt is positive. The best explanation for this observation is that

(A) It is impossible to predict the relationship between the two compounds.
(B) There is resonance present in the carboxylate ion.
(C) There is an increase in the molecular weight when sodium replaces hydrogen.
(D) The change from a neutral molecule to an ion reverses the optical activity.

99. The following compound was isolated from a reaction:

OH

How many stereoisomers are possible for this compound?

(A) 2
(B) 4
(C) 8
(D) 16

100. Carbohydrates can normally exist in the form of several stereoisomers. The number of carbohydrate stereoisomers, with n = chiral carbon atoms and m = meso forms, is equal to

(A) 2^n
(B) $2n$
(C) $2n + m$
(D) $2^n + m$

101. Which of the following is NOT true about diastereomers?

(A) They may have different melting points.
(B) The molecular formulas may be different.
(C) The optical rotations may be different.
(D) The gas chromatography retention times may be different.

102. Compounds C and D are enantiomers. Compound D was found to have an R absolute configuration and a positive optical rotation. Compound C has the following absolute configuration and optical rotation

(A) R, positive
(B) S, positive
(C) R, negative
(D) S, negative

103. A chemist is investigating a new reaction on cyclohexane. She reasons that there are two possible products. These products are

Which of the following properties is most likely NOT the same for each of the two possible products?

(A) optical activity
(B) boiling point
(C) solubility in water
(D) All of the properties would be different.

104. What is the stereochemistry of this cyclic amine?

(A) 2R and 3S
(B) 2S and 3R
(C) 2S and 3S
(D) 2R and 3R

105. For which of the following molecules is hydrogen bonding an important factor influencing the physical properties?

I   II   III   IV

(A) I, II, III, and IV
(B) I, III, and IV
(C) II, III, and IV
(D) III and IV

106. What are the absolute configurations of the following compounds?

I   II

(A) I is R, and II is S
(B) I is R, and II is R
(C) I is S, and II is S
(D) I is S, and II is R

107. What is the relationship between the following two molecules?

	CHO				CHO	
HO		H		HO		H
H		OH		H		Cl
Cl		H		HO		H
H		OH		H		OH
	CH₂OH				CH₂OH	

(A) enantiomers
(B) regioisomers
(C) conformers
(D) identical

108. Which of the following molecules are meso compounds?

I

II

III

IV

(A) II and III
(B) III and IV
(C) I and III
(D) I and IV

109. How are the boiling points of the following compounds related?

I

II

III

(A) III > II > I
(B) II > III > I
(C) III > I > II
(D) I > III > II

110. What is the best explanation of why compound I has a higher boiling point than compound II?

I   II

(A) Compound I can ionize.
(B) Compound II is nonpolar.
(C) Compound I has hydrogen bonding.
(D) Compound II is unstable.

111. Which of the following compounds has an internal plane of symmetry?

I   II   III   IV

(A) I only
(B) III and IV
(C) II only
(D) none

112. Which of the following molecules is achiral?

(A)

(B)

(C)

(D)

113. An unknown substance has an optical rotation of 0° and a sharp melting point. The unknown substance reacts with the S stereoisomer of another compound to produce two easily separated products with different melting points. Which of the following could describe the unknown substance?

(A) It is a racemic mixture.
(B) It is a cis isomer.
(C) It is an equimolar mixture of two diastereomers.
(D) It has two different compounds present.

114. How many optical isomers does cholesterol have? The structure of cholesterol is

(A) 512
(B) 128
(C) 64
(D) 256

115. The drug thalidomide was introduced in the late 1950s to alleviate the morning sickness that often accompanies pregnancy. Synthesis of the drug resulted in a racemic mixture. One of the enantiomers was the active ingredient for treating morning sickness, while the other enantiomer led to birth defects. The following is one of the enantiomers of thalidomide. What is the absolute configuration of this enantiomer?

(A) R
(B) S
(C) (+)
(D) (–)

116. Which of the following cyclopropanes is a meso compound?

(A)

(B)

(C)

(D)

CHAPTER 3

Substitution and Elimination Reactions

117. The monochlorination of methylpropane gives 64% 1-chloro-2-methylpropane and 36% 2-chloro-2-methylpropane. What is the approximate selectivity ratio of 3° to 1° in the reaction?

(A) 64:36

(B) 36:64

(C) 1:9

(D) 5:1

118. An organic chemist uses the following reaction to produce the starting material for another reaction. The reaction takes place in dry ether and gives one organic product.

What is the major product of this reaction?

(A)

(B)

(C)

(D)

119. It is possible to form an ether through the reaction of an alkoxide with a primary alkyl halide. The alkoxide functions as

(A) an electrophile
(B) a nucleophile
(C) an acid
(D) a catalyst

120. How many products form in the monochlorination of 2-methylbutane?

(A) 12
(B) 8
(C) 4
(D) 1

121. An organic chemist investigates the following reaction.

What is the major product?

(A)

(B)

(C)

(D)

122. An organic chemist investigates the following reaction.

$$\xrightarrow[\text{H}_2\text{SO}_4]{\text{K}_2\text{Cr}_2\text{O}_7}$$

What is the major product?

(A)

(B)

(C)

(D)

123. An organic chemist investigates the following reaction.

Which of the following is the most likely reaction intermediate?

(A)

(B)

(C)

(D)

124. When plotting an S$_N$2 mechanism on a reaction coordinate graph, which of the following would be at the highest point on the graph?

(A)

(B)

(C)

(D)

125. Which of the following is the best leaving group?

(A) OH$^-$

(B) CH$_3$O$^-$

(C) NH$_3$

(D) NH$_2^-$

126. Which of the following leads to the best leaving group?

(A) C-N=NH

(B) C-NH-NH$_2$

(C) C-NH$_2$

(D) C-$^+$N≡N

127. Which of the following illustrates a propagation step in a free radical chain reaction?

(A) $:\ddot{\underset{..}{Cl}}\cdot$ +   (isopropyl CH with CH₃, CH₃, CH₃)   ⟶   (tert-butyl radical with CH₃, CH₃, CH₃)   + HCl

(B) $2:\ddot{\underset{..}{Cl}}\cdot \longrightarrow :\ddot{\underset{..}{Cl}} — \ddot{\underset{..}{Cl}}:$

(C) (tert-butyl radical with CH₃, CH₃, CH₃)   + $:\ddot{\underset{..}{Cl}}\cdot$ ⟶ (tert-butyl chloride with CH₃, CH₃, CH₃, Cl)

(D) $:\ddot{\underset{..}{Cl}} — \ddot{\underset{..}{Cl}}: \xrightarrow{h\nu} 2\cdot\ddot{\underset{..}{Cl}}:$

128. Which of the following free radicals is the most stable?

(A) (benzene ring with C(CH₃)₂ radical)

(B) (benzene ring with radical on ring, isopropyl substituent)

(C) (benzene ring with CH radical bearing CH₃ and CH₃)

(D) (benzene ring with radical on ring, isopropyl substituent)

129. An organic chemist investigates the following reaction.

$$\underset{\underset{CH_3}{|}}{\overset{CH_3}{|}}CH \quad + \quad Cl_2 \quad \longrightarrow \quad \underset{\underset{Cl}{|}}{\overset{CH_3}{|}}C$$

Which of the following intermediates is most likely to be important to the reaction?

(A) $\underset{CH_3}{\overset{CH_3}{|}}Cl \text{----} C \text{-----} H$, with CH_3

(B) $\overset{CH_3}{|}$ C with CH_3, H, $\dot{C}H_2$

(C) $\overset{CH_3}{|}$ C$\oplus$ with CH_3, CH_3

(D) $\overset{CH_3}{|}$ $\dot{C}$ with CH_3, CH_3

130. Which of the following molecules is most likely to react via an S_N2 mechanism?

(A)

(B)

(C)

(D)

131. Which of the following alcohols CANNOT be oxidized to a carbonyl compound by acidic $K_2Cr_2O_7$?

(A) CH_3OH

(B)

(C)

(D)

132. Which of the following alcohols will most likely react with HBr through an S_N1 mechanism?

I   II

III   IV

(A) I and III
(B) II and IV
(C) III and IV
(D) II and III

133. Which of the following is the major product from the dehydration of 2-methyl-1-pentanol?

I   II   III

(A) I
(B) II
(C) III
(D) All form in equal amounts.

134. Which of the following is the major product formed by the free radical bromination of isopentane?

(A)

(B)

(C)

(D)

135. Why is structure II more stable than structure I?

$$CH_3-\underset{\underset{CH_3}{|}}{\overset{\overset{CH_3}{|}}{C}}-CH_3 \qquad CH_3-\underset{\underset{CH_3}{|}}{\overset{\overset{CH_3}{|}}{C}}-CH_3$$

I II

(A) The two groups can be axial, so there is less repulsion.
(B) The two groups can be equatorial, so there is less repulsion.
(C) The t-butyl group can be axial, so there is less repulsion with the equatorial ethyl group.
(D) The t-butyl group can be equatorial, so there is less repulsion with the axial ethyl group.

136. Which of the following molecules is the better nucleophile, H–S⁻ or H–Se⁻?

(A) H–Se⁻
(B) H–S⁻
(C) It is not possible to tell.
(D) They are the same.

137. The acetate ion is a stronger base than the trichloroacetate ion. Why is it a stronger base?

(A) inductive effects
(B) higher polarity
(C) resonance effects
(D) steric hindrance

138. Place the following carbocations in order of increasing stability.

I   II   III

(A) I < III < II
(B) II < I < III
(C) II < III < I
(D) I < II < III

139. The reaction of a certain alkyl bromide utilizes a carbocation intermediate. The carbon in the carbocation has what type of hybridization?

(A) sp^3
(B) sp^2
(C) sp
(D) p^3

140. The product(s) of an S_N1 reaction by an achiral molecule on a molecule with a chiral center produces

(A) a racemic mixture
(B) an inversion of configuration
(C) a retention of configuration
(D) an achiral product

141. An S_N2 mechanism does NOT include

(A) second-order kinetics
(B) a one-step mechanism
(C) a five-coordinate intermediate
(D) a carbocation intermediate

142. An E1 mechanism does NOT include

(A) first-order kinetics
(B) attack by a nucleophile on a carbocation
(C) the formation of a π bond
(D) a two-step mechanism

143. An E2 mechanism does NOT include

(A) two carbon atoms changing from sp^3 to sp^2 hybridization
(B) the formation of a π bond
(C) the formation of a carbocation intermediate
(D) the loss of a leaving group

144. The chlorination of an alkane is a(n)

(A) free radical reaction
(B) S_N1 reaction
(C) S_N2 reaction
(D) E2 reaction

145. The study of an S_N2 reaction on an alkyl halide utilizing hydroxide ion as the nucleophile showed a dependence upon the solvent. If the solvent lowers the reaction rate, the solvent

(A) destabilizes the nucleophile
(B) decreases the activation energy
(C) increases the value of the rate constant
(D) solvates the nucleophile more effectively

146. The study of a series of alkyl halides with the general formula RR'R"C-X, where the different R's may or may not be the same and X is Cl, Br, or I, found that the rate of the S_N2 reaction decreased with an increase in the average size of the R groups. Why did the rate decrease?

(A) There is an increase in the stability of the product.
(B) There is a loss of optical activity.
(C) There is an increase in the activation energy.
(D) The mechanism shifts from S_N2 to S_N1.

147. The reaction of methyl bromide, under nucleophilic substitution conditions, most likely illustrates

(A) second-order kinetics
(B) the formation of a racemic mixture
(C) retention of configuration
(D) first-order kinetics

148. Which of the following illustrates a termination step in a free radical chain reaction?

(A)

(B)

(C)

(D)

149. An S_N2 mechanism does NOT include

(A) the reactivity sequence $1° > 2° > 3°$
(B) inversion of configuration
(C) no rearrangement
(D) first-order kinetics

150. One experiment in the investigation of the reaction of ethyl iodide with hydroxide ion found that doubling the concentration of hydroxide ion caused the rate to

(A) quadruple
(B) double
(C) remain the same
(D) triple

151. The main difference between the rate law for an S_N1 mechanism and an S_N2 mechanism is that the rate law for an S_N1 process depends only on

(A) the concentration of the substrate
(B) the concentration of the nucleophile
(C) the concentration of the solvent
(D) pressure

152. Which of the following is true concerning an S_N2 mechanism?

(A) The concentration of the nucleophile is not important.
(B) It is a two-step process.
(C) There is retention of configuration.
(D) Primary alkyl halides react faster than secondary or tertiary alkyl halides.

153. The free radical chlorination of an alkane is best described as

(A) nonregioselective leading to a number of isomers due to inductive and statistical factors
(B) nonregioselective leading to the most stable isomer due to inductive and statistical factors
(C) stereoselective producing primarily one enantiomer
(D) nonstereoselective producing a racemic mixture of the two enantiomers

154. What is the name of the first step in a free radical halogenation mechanism?

(A) initiation
(B) commencement
(C) instigation
(D) propagation

155. What is the best explanation of why CH_3CH_2Cl reacts via an S_N2 mechanism faster than $CH_3CH_2CH_2CH_2Cl$?

(A) The ethyl group leads to less steric interference.
(B) Ethyl chloride has a lower boiling point than butyl chloride.
(C) Ethyl chloride interacts less with the solvent.
(D) The ethyl group stabilizes the intermediate carbocation better.

156. The R form of the following compound will react with a mixture of NaI in acetone

What is the major product of the reaction?

(A) a racemic mixture of 3-iodo-2,3-dimethylpentane
(B) (R)-3-iodo-2,3-dimethylpentane
(C) (S)-3-iodo-2,3-dimethylpentane
(D) 2,3,3-trimethylpentane

157. What are the products of the room temperature reaction of one equivalent of hydrogen chloride gas and one equivalent of 1,3-butadiene?

(A) 3-chloro-1-butene plus 1-chloro-2-butene
(B) 2-chloro-1-butene plus 1-chloro-2-butene
(C) 2-chloro-1-butene plus 2-chloro-2-butene
(D) 1-chloro-1-butene plus 1-chloro-2-butene

158. Which molecule is the better nucleophile, OH^- or NH_2^-?

(A) OH^-
(B) NH_2^-
(C) It is not possible to tell.
(D) They are the same.

159. What is the product of the reaction of 2-hexene with $CHCl_3$ in the presence of potassium t-butoxide?

(A)

Cl

Cl

(B)

CCl_3

(C)

t-OBu

(D)

Cl

Cl

160. What is the purpose of the propoxide ion in the following reaction?

Cl

^-OPr
$\xrightarrow{PrOH}$

OPr

(A) This is an S_N2 reaction, and the propoxide ion is the nucleophile.
(B) This is an S_N2 reaction, and the propoxide ion is the electrophile.
(C) This is an S_N1 reaction, and the propoxide ion is the base.
(D) This is an S_N1 reaction, and the propoxide ion is the electrophile.

161. An organic chemist examined a number of reactions involving an S_N2 mechanism and found the decrease in rate with increased size of the primary alkyl halide. In addition, there was a decrease in the rate with an increase in the branching on the alkyl halide. This information leads to additional information concerning

(A) the steric effects on this reaction
(B) the increased stability of larger alkyls
(C) the high reactivity of alkyl halides
(D) the decrease in polarity of larger alkyl halides

162. The free radical monobromination of methylcyclopentane only forms the following product

The best explanation for this observation is

(A) the stabilization of the intermediate through resonance
(B) the attack occurs at the least sterically hindered site
(C) the stabilization of the intermediate through inductive effects
(D) the attack occurs at the site that is the most δ+

163. In a free radical addition reaction, all propagation steps involve the reaction of

(A) a molecule to produce two free radicals
(B) a free radical to produce a free radical
(C) two free radicals to produce a molecule
(D) a free radical to produce a carbocation

164. In the presence of sodium ethoxide, 3-chloro-3-ethylpentane reacts primarily by an S_N1 mechanism instead of an S_N2 mechanism. Doubling the concentration of sodium ethoxide causes

(A) a decrease in the rate of reaction
(B) an increase in the rate of reaction
(C) no change in the rate of reaction
(D) a change from an S_N1 to an S_N2 mechanism

165. The carbocation formed by the reaction of an unknown alkyl bromide is more stable than the carbocation formed by the reaction of neopentyl bromide. The unknown alkyl bromide might be

(A) isopropyl bromide
(B) ethyl bromide
(C) methyl bromide
(D) propyl bromide

166. Which of the following compounds is the most likely to react via an S_N1 mechanism?

(A) CH_3CH_2I
(B) $(CH_3)_3CCH_2I$
(C) $(CH_3)_2CHI$
(D) $(CH_3)_3CI$

167. Place the following free radicals in order of decreasing stability.

| I | II | III | IV |

(A) III > II > IV > I
(B) III > II ≈ IV > I
(C) I > IV > II > III
(D) I > III > IV > II

168. Phenol is a weak acid. Which of the following benzene-ring substituents will increase its strength as an acid?

$$-CN \qquad -CH_2CH_3 \qquad -CCl_3$$
$$\text{I} \qquad\qquad \text{II} \qquad\qquad \text{III}$$

(A) I and III
(B) I and II
(C) II and III
(D) I, II, and III

169. Which of the following is the most stable conformation of 1,2-ethandiol? (The remaining hydrogen atoms have been removed for clarity.)

| I | II | III |

(A) I
(B) II
(C) III
(D) All are equal.

170. Which of the following are the products formed by the free radical chlorination of isopentane?

I   II   III   IV

(A) I, II, III, and IV
(B) II and IV
(C) I and III
(D) I, II, and III

171. Which of the following alcohols will most likely react with HBr through an S_N2 mechanism?

I   II

III   IV

(A) III and IV
(B) I and III
(C) II and IV
(D) II and III

172. What is the major product of the following reaction?

(A)

(B)

(C)

(D) no reaction

173. An organic chemist investigates the following reaction in the presence of light.

+ Br$_2$ ⟶

Which of the following will be the major product?

(A)

(B)

(C)

(D)

174. An organic chemist investigates the following reaction.

Which of the following will be the major product?

I

II

III

IV

(A) I only
(B) II only
(C) I and II
(D) III and IV

175. An organic chemist investigates the following reaction.

$$\xrightarrow[\text{CH}_2\text{Cl}_2]{\text{PBr}_3}$$

Which of the following will be the major product?

(A)

OPO_3

(B)

Br

(C)

(D)

Br

176. Which of the following nitrogen-containing species will NOT serve as a nucleophile?

(A)

$$\text{R} - \overset{\displaystyle |}{\underset{\displaystyle \text{H}}{\text{N}}} - \text{H}$$

(B)

$$\text{R} - \overset{\displaystyle \text{R}}{\underset{\displaystyle \text{R}}{\overset{\oplus}{\text{N}}}} - \text{R}$$

(C)

$$\text{R} - \overset{\displaystyle |}{\underset{\displaystyle \text{R}}{\text{N}}} - \text{H}$$

(D)

$$\text{R} - \overset{\displaystyle |}{\underset{\displaystyle \text{R}}{\text{N}}} - \text{R}$$

177. The reaction of t-butyl iodide with formate ion occurs more rapidly in aqueous solution than in DMF solutions. Why is this the case?

(A) DMF reacts with the formate ion.
(B) Water is smaller, which leads to less steric hindrance.
(C) Water stabilizes the intermediate carbocation better.
(D) DMF forms a less reactive intermediate.

178. A chemist is investigating the following type of reaction using primary and secondary alcohols. After mixing the reactants, the mixture is refluxed.

$$ROH + SOCl_2 \rightarrow$$

What type of compound is the most likely product?

(A)
```
        O
        ||
R—O—S—OH
        ||
        O
```

(B)
```
        O
       //
R—S
       \
        O
```

(C) R—Cl

(D)
```
R—S
     \
      H
```

179. It is possible to dehydrate an alcohol by heating the alcohol with phosphoric acid. Which of the following alcohols would undergo dehydration most rapidly?

(A)

(B)

(C)

(D)

CHAPTER 4

Electrophilic Addition Reactions

180. Sulfonation of toluene produces p-toluenesulfonic acid and o-toluene-sulfonic acid. What is the relationship between these two products?

(A) anomers
(B) conformers
(C) constitutional isomers
(D) diastereomers

181. The following illustrates a generic Diels-Alder reaction.

What is the net change in the number of σ and π bonds?

(A) − 2 π and + 2 σ
(B) − 2 π and + 3 σ
(C) − 3 π and + 3 σ
(D) − 3 π and + 2 σ

182. Hydrogen bromide will react with $CH_3\text{-}CH=CH\text{-}CH=CH\text{-}CH_2CH_2CH_3$. What is the reaction intermediate?

(A) a conjugate base
(B) a carbanion
(C) a free radical
(D) a carbonium ion

183. Hydrogen halides will add to an alkene. Which halide reacts most rapidly with an alkene in a nonpolar, aprotic solvent?

(A) HBr
(B) HI
(C) HCl
(D) HF

184. An organic chemist investigated the following reaction and isolated two products.

What was the structure of the major product?

(A)

(B)

(C)

OH

(D)

OC(CH$_3$)$_3$

185. Rank the following in increasing order of reactivity rate with Br$_2$/FeBr$_3$.

I   II   III

(A) II < I < III
(B) I < II < III
(C) II < III < I
(D) III < II < I

186. The following reaction produces one major product.

$$Cl_2/FeCl_3$$

What is the structure of the major product?

(A)

(B)

(C)

(D)

187. It is possible to produce mostly one alkyl halide via the following reaction.

HCl

What is the structure of the major product?

(A)

(B)

(C)

(D)

188. What is the major product of the reaction of bromine in carbon tetrachloride with cyclohexene?

(A) racemic 1,2-dibromocyclohexane
(B) meso 1,2-dibromocyclohexane
(C) 1,1-dibromocyclohexane
(D) 1-bromocyclohexane

189. Which of the following is the major product of the reaction of trans-2-butene with meta-chloroperoxybenzoic acid (mCPBA) in methylene chloride?

(A)

(B)

(C)

(D)

190. A chemist conducts the following two-step chemical procedure.

What is the major product of the reaction?

(A)

(B)

(C)

(D)

191. A chemist conducts the following two-step chemical procedure.

1) B_2H_6/THF
2) H_2O_2/NaOH/H_2O

What is the major product of the reaction?

(A)

OH

OH

(B)

OH

(C)

OH

(D)

192. A chemist conducts the following two-step chemical procedure.

1) O_3

1) Zn/HOAc

What is one of the major product(s) of the reaction?

(A)

(B)

(C)

(D)

193. The following reaction produces one major product.

H_2

Lindlar Catalyst

What is the major product of the reaction?

(A)

(B)

(C)

(D)

194. The following reaction produces one major product.

$$SO_3/H_2SO_4$$

What is the major product of the reaction?

(A)

(B)

(C)

(D)

195. The following reaction produces one major product.

What is the major product of the reaction?

(A)

(B)

(C)

(D)

196. Assuming all molecules are planar, which of the following is NOT aromatic?

(A)

(B)

(C)

(D)

197. Which of the following species is NOT aromatic?

(A)

(B)

(C)

(D)

198. Which of the following is the major product formed by the reaction of aqueous bromine with 2-methylpropene?

(A) I
(B) II
(C) III
(D) I and II

199. Which product(s) form from the reaction of benzoic acid with a mixture of nitric and sulfuric acids?

(A)

COOH
[benzene ring with NO₂ at para position]
NO₂

(B)

COOH
[benzene ring with NO₂ at ortho and para positions]
NO₂
NO₂

(C)

COOH
[benzene ring with O₂N at meta position]
O₂N

(D)

COOH
[benzene ring with O₂N and OSO₃ substituents]
O₂N   OSO₃

200. Where does substitution occur when nitrobenzene reacts with a hot mixture of Br_2 and $FeBr_3$?

(A) meta
(B) ortho
(C) para
(D) ortho and para

201. The addition of hydrogen bromide in the presence of peroxide to 1-pentene could form either of the products shown below.

I   II

How do the relative amounts of the two products compare?

(A) I predominates
(B) II predominates
(C) equal amount of each
(D) the external pressure

202. The hydrogenation of the following compound using a Lindlar catalyst will form what type of compound?

(A) an alkane
(B) an alkene
(C) an alkyne
(D) a cyclic compound

203. Which of the following are formed by the reaction of meta-chloroperoxybenzoic acid (mCPBA) with 4-methylcyclohexene, followed by treatment with base?

I   II   III   IV

(A) I and III
(B) II and III
(C) III and IV
(D) I and II

204. Which of the following are formed by the reaction of basic permanganate with cyclohexene?

I   II   III   IV

(A) II only
(B) I and III
(C) IV only
(D) II and IV

205. The following molecule is the starting material for the Markovnikov addition of water. What is the best description of the intermediate formed in the first step of the reaction mechanism?

(A) a tertiary carbonium ion
(B) a secondary carbonium ion
(C) a tertiary carbanion
(D) a secondary carbanion

206. The addition of hydrogen bromide to 1-butene produces 2-bromobutane. The two products isolated are

What is the best description of the products?
(A) conformers
(B) diastereomers
(C) enantiomers
(D) structural isomers

207. The addition of hydrogen bromide to 1-butene produces 2-bromobutane. The two products isolated in equal amounts are

What is the specific rotation of the product mixture?
(A) 0°
(B) +15°
(C) −15°
(D) impossible to determine

208. The addition reaction of HBr with an alkene is

(A) a one-step process
(B) an anti-Markovnikov reaction
(C) initiated by nucleophilic attack
(D) a two-step process

209. Alkenes will undergo addition reactions with compounds such as HBr. In the presence of peroxides, the mechanism involves

(A) an sp intermediate
(B) no initiation step
(C) the formation of a Markovnikov product
(D) the formation of an anti-Markovnikov product

210. The low reactivity of aromatic systems toward electrophilic substitution occurs because the aromatic system is

(A) a poor nucleophile
(B) a poor electrophile
(C) nonpolar
(D) very reactive

211. The hydration of an alkene is an acid-catalyzed reaction that yields the Markovnikov alcohol. The acid behaves as a catalyst because

(A) it reacts in a 1:1 ratio with the alkene
(B) it increases the activation energy
(C) the reaction will proceed without the acid
(D) it decreases the heat of reaction

212. The exhaustive nitration of toluene yields 2,4,6-trinitrotoluene, better known as TNT. The formula of TNT is $C_7H_5N_3O_6$. The hybridization of the nitrogen atoms is

(A) only sp^3
(B) some sp^2 and some sp^3
(C) only sp^2
(D) some sp and some sp^2

213. Which of the following reagents would convert the following compound to 2-bromo-2-methylbutane?

$$CH_3 \quad\quad CH_3$$
$$\underset{H}{\overset{}{C}}=\underset{CH_3}{\overset{}{C}}$$

(A) Br_2
(B) HBr
(C) $Br_2 + H_2O$
(D) HBr + peroxide

214. The mononitration of toluene yields a mixture of 2-nitrotoluene and 4-nitrotoluene. The formula of both compounds is $C_7H_7NO_2$. Both of these products may undergo further nitration to form dinitro and trini-tro products. Further nitration requires a different temperature than the mononitration. The temperature and explanation is

(A) higher temperature because the first nitro group is ring deactivating
(B) higher temperature because the first nitro group is ring activating
(C) lower temperature because the first nitro group is ring deactivating
(D) lower temperature because the first nitro group is ring activating

215. An organic chemist wishes to produce chloroheptane by the reaction of hydrogen chloride with cis-3-heptene. What would be the best solvent for this reaction?

(A) cis-3-heptene
(B) EtOH
(C) CHOOH
(D) H_2O

216. Which of the following dienophiles would react most rapidly with cyclopentadiene via a Diels-Alder reaction?

(A)
$$CH_3$$
$$\underset{CH_3}{\overset{}{\underset{}{CH}}}-CH=CH-\underset{CH_3}{\overset{CH_3}{CH}}$$

(B) $CH_3-CH=CH-O-CH_3$

(C) $CH_3-CH=CH-CH_3$

(D)
$$CH_3-CH=CH-\underset{\underset{O}{\overset{\|}{}}}{C}-CH_3$$

217. An organic chemist conducts the following reaction

$$\xrightarrow{\text{NaNH}_2/\text{NH}_3}$$

What was the major product?

(A)

(B)

(C)

(D)

218. Which of the following compounds form from the reaction of 1-methylcyclohexene with B_2H_6 and H_2O_2/OH^-?

(A)

(B)

(C)

(D)

219. An organic chemist conducts four experiments on $CH_2=CH-C(CH_3)_3$. Which of the following reactions will lead to a change in the carbon backbone?

(A) H_2SO_4/H_2O
(B) B_2H_6/heat
(C) Pt/H_2
(D) HBr/benzoyl peroxide

220. Which of the following compounds would undergo sulfonation to produce the highest para-to-ortho sulfonic acid ratio?

(A) toluene
(B) isopropylbenzene
(C) t-butylbenzene
(D) ethylbenzene

221. An organic chemist treats the following compound with ozone and then treats the products with a zinc/water mixture. How many different products form?

(A) 4
(B) 3
(C) 2
(D) 1

222. The reaction of HCl with Z-3-methyl-3-heptene is most likely

(A) syn- and anti-addition to give the Markovnikov products
(B) anti-addition to give the Markovnikov product
(C) syn- and anti-addition to give the anti-Markovnikov products
(D) anti-addition to give the anti-Markovnikov product

223. Which of the following undergoes chlorination the fastest in the presence of $Cl_2/FeCl_3$?

(A)

(B)

(C)

(D)

224. Electron-withdrawing groups deactivate aromatic rings toward reaction via electrophilic aromatic substitution. However, these same groups promote nucleophilic aromatic substitution. Which of the following is the best explanation for this observation?

(A) resonance
(B) steric hindrance
(C) stabilization of the free radical
(D) stabilization of the carbocation

225. Grignard reagents, such as $CH_3CH_2CH_2MgBr$, will react with carbonyl groups. Which of the following will react with a Grignard reagent to produce a secondary alcohol?

(A)

(B)

(C)

(D)

226. For most addition reactions of an alkene with a hydrogen halide, HX, the rate law is: rate = k[HX] [alkene]. This rate law indicates all of the following EXCEPT

(A) The reaction is first order with respect to the alkene.
(B) The reaction is second order overall.
(C) The rate-determining step involves one molecule of HX and one molecule of the alkene.
(D) The reaction occurs in a single step involving one molecule of HX and one molecule of the alkene.

227. When an aromatic compound undergoes electrophilic aromatic substitution, the aromatic substrate is the

(A) nucleophile
(B) electrophile
(C) dienophile
(D) intermediate

228. The mononitration of toluene yields a mixture of 2-nitrotoluene and 4-nitrotoluene. The formula of both compounds is $C_7H_7NO_2$. The two products are examples of

(A) conformers
(B) enantiomers
(C) constitutional isomers
(D) geometric isomers

229. Alkenes will undergo an acid-catalyzed addition of water. This reaction involves all of the following EXCEPT

(A) a carbocation intermediate
(B) an anti-Markovnikov product
(C) the formation of an alcohol
(D) the initial protonation of the double bond

230. The addition of hydrogen bromide to 1-butene produces 2-bromobutane. The two products isolated in equal amounts are

Which of the following is NOT true about the reaction?

(A) The result of the reaction is a racemic mixture.
(B) The rate-determining step in the mechanism is the formation of a carbocation.
(C) The overall rate law is second order.
(D) It is possible to separate the products by fractional distillation.

231. One reaction of alkenes is ozonolysis. The reaction sequence begins with the reaction with ozone and ends with a treatment of the ozonide formed with zinc and water. How many different products will the ozonolysis of the following compound yield?

(A) 2
(B) 5
(C) 3
(D) 4

232. The addition of hydrogen bromide to 1-pentene could form either of the following products

How do the relative amounts of the two products compare?
(A) I only
(B) II only
(C) equal amount of each
(D) the distribution depends upon the temperature

233. The addition of bromine in carbon tetrachloride to 1-pentene forms 1,2-dibromopentane
(A) as a meso compound
(B) as a syn-addition product
(C) as an enantiomer of the reactant
(D) as a racemic mixture

234. The following reaction produces one major product

$$\xrightarrow{\text{D}_2/\text{Ni}}$$

What is the major product of the reaction?

(A)

(B)

(C)

(D)

235. The following reaction produces one major product

$$\xrightarrow[\text{2) H}_2\text{O}]{\text{1) Na/NH}_3(1)}$$

What is the major product of the reaction?

(A)

(B)

(C)

(D)

236. The following reaction produces one major product

What is the major product of the reaction?

(A)

(B)

(C)

(D)

237. An organic chemist is studying the following Diels-Alder reaction.

What is the major product?

(A)

(B)

(C)

(D)

238. Sodium cyanide will react with propyl bromide at room temperature. An organic chemist does two experiments, each with equal amounts of the two reactants. In one experiment, 100 mL of solvent is present and the reaction takes 10 minutes to go to completion. In the second experiment, 50 mL of solvent is used. How long will it take the second reaction to go to completion?

(A) 5 minutes
(B) 2.5 minutes
(C) 10 minutes
(D) 7.5 minutes

239. What type of intermediate should form during the Markovnikov addition of HBr to the following compound?

(A) a secondary carbanion
(B) a secondary carbonium ion
(C) a tertiary carbanion
(D) a tertiary carbonium ion

240. The hydration of an alkene may lead to two different compounds. These compounds are

(A) tautomers
(B) conformers
(C) regioisomers
(D) anomers

241. An organic chemistry student investigates the following reaction in lab.

$$\xrightarrow{\text{HNO}_3/\text{H}_2\text{SO}_4}$$

Which of the following is the major product?

(A)

(B)

(C)

(D)

242. An organic chemistry student performs the following experiment in lab.

What is the purpose of the zinc amalgam, Zn(Hg)?

(A) It is a reducing agent.
(B) It is an oxidizing agent.
(C) It is a catalyst.
(D) It is a Lewis base.

CHAPTER 5

Nucleophilic and Cyclo Addition Reactions

243. What type of compound will form as a result of the following reaction?

(A) an ether
(B) a hemiacetal
(C) an acetal
(D) a carboxylic acid

244. What is the name of the process where an aldehyde or ketone is in equilibrium with its enol form?

(A) mutarotation
(B) inversion of configuration
(C) tautomerism
(D) hydrolysis

245. While investigating the following chemical reaction, an organic chemist found that one product formed in a 95% yield.

What was the structure of the one product formed?

(A)

(B)

(C)

(D)

246. While investigating the following chemical reaction, an organic chemist found that one product formed in a 75% yield.

What was the structure of the one product formed?

(A)

(B)

(C)

(D)

247. While investigating the following chemical reaction, an organic chemist found that one product formed in a 95% yield.

What was the structure of the one product formed?

(A)

(B)

(C)

(D)

248. An organic chemist was investigating the following reaction.

NaOH/H₂O

What was the structure of one of the organic products?

(A)

(B)

(C)

(D)

249. An organic chemist was investigating the following reaction.

What was the structure of the major product?

(A)

(B)

(C)

(D)

250. It is possible to generate a carboxylic acid through the acid hydrolysis of an ester. Which of the following esters would produce 3-methylpentanoic acid upon acid hydrolysis?

(A)

(B)

(C)

(D)

251. It is possible to oxidize many alcohols to carboxylic acids by oxidation with acidic potassium dichromate. This method of synthesis will work for which of the following alcohols?

(A) OH

(B) OH

(C) OH

(D) OH

252. It is possible to reduce 3-methylbutanoic acid with LiAlH$_4$. The product
of the LiAlH$_4$ reaction will react with additional 3-methylbutanoic acid, in
the presence of an acid catalyst, to produce a new compound. What is the
structure of the new compound?

(A)

(B)

(C)

(D)

253. Which of the following is the strongest acid?

(A)

(B)

(C)

(D)

254. In organic synthesis, it is possible to replace acid chlorides with acid bromides. What is the advantage of using the more expensive acid bromide?

(A) It is easier to separate the products.
(B) The large bromide ion minimizes side reactions.
(C) The bromide released catalyzes further reaction.
(D) Acid bromides are more reactive.

255. Which of the following compounds contains a hemiacetal?

(A)

    —OH

(B)

    —O—CH$_3$

(C)

(D)

256. What is the best explanation why acyl halides react by addition-elimination reactions while aldehydes and ketones undergo nucleophilic addition reactions?

(A) They are stronger electrophiles.
(B) The halide ions are good leaving groups.
(C) They are more polar.
(D) The carbonyl group is more reactive.

257. Which of the following is a characteristic of hemiacetal formation through the reaction of an alcohol with an aldehyde?

(A) The transition-state is 5-coordinate.
(B) It has a carbocation intermediate.
(C) It is a stereospecific reaction.
(D) It follows second-order kinetics.

258. What is the major product of the reaction of excess propanal with aqueous base at 0-10°C?

(A)

(B)

(C)

(D)

259. The reaction of the enolate anion of a carbonyl compound with another carbonyl compound is

(A) an aldol condensation
(B) an esterification
(C) a saponification
(D) a neutralization

260. Rank the following acids in order of increasing acidity.

I   II   III   IV

(A) III < I < IV < II
(B) IV < III < I < II
(C) I = III < II < IV
(D) II < I < III < IV

261. An acetal can be formed by the reaction of a
(A) ketone plus an aldehyde
(B) carboxylic acid plus an alcohol
(C) carboxylic acid plus an acetate ion
(D) ketone plus an alcohol

262. Which of the following compounds is the strongest acid?

(A)

(B)

(C)

(D)

263. What happens when an aldehyde and a dilute acid are mixed?
(A) A hydroxy aldehyde forms through an aldol condensation.
(B) A carboxylic acid forms through oxidation.
(C) A ketone forms through a nucleophilic attack followed by oxidation.
(D) A carboxylic acid forms through tautomerism.

264. The base-catalyzed hydrolysis of an amide will produce which of the following?

(A) an imide and an aldehyde
(B) an amine and a carboxylic acid
(C) an amine and a carboxylate ion
(D) an ammonium ion and a carboxylate ion

265. The following is an example of an aldol addition:

$$CH_3-C(=O)-H \xrightarrow[5°C]{10\% \ NaOH/H_2O} CH_3-CH(OH)-CH_2-C(=O)-H$$

What is the role of the NaOH in this reaction?

(A) deprotonation
(B) protonation
(C) electrophile
(D) termination

266. What type of compound is the major product of the following reaction?

$$R-C(=O)-O-C(=O)-R + HO-C(R')(R'') \longrightarrow$$

(A) a diketone
(B) a ketone
(C) an aldehyde
(D) an ester

267. Which of the following compounds will NOT react with a very strong base such as potassium t-butoxide?

(A)

(B)

(C)

(D)

268. What is the first step in an aldol condensation under basic conditions?

    (A) removal of the α-hydrogen
    (B) protonation of a carbonyl group
    (C) reaction of the enol
    (D) addition of base to the carbonyl

269. What is the best procedure for the following reaction?

    (A) $NaBH_4$/MeOH 25°
    (B) $ZnCl_2$/HCl
    (C) 1) $LiAlH_4$ 2) HCl
    (D) 1) B_2H_6 2) H_2O_2/OH⁻

270. Which of the following acids is the easiest to decarboxylate?

(A)

(B)

(C)

(D)

271. What is the major product of the reaction of excess ethylmagnesium bromide with ethyl butanoate followed by acid workup?

(A)
$$Pr-\underset{\underset{OEt}{|}}{\overset{\overset{Et}{|}}{C}}-OEt$$

(B)
$$Pr-\underset{\overset{\|}{O}}{C}-Et$$

(C)
$$Pr-\underset{\underset{OH}{|}}{\overset{\overset{Et}{|}}{C}}-Et$$

(D)
$$Pr-\underset{\underset{OH}{|}}{\overset{\overset{Et}{|}}{C}}-OEt$$

272. Which of the following is part of the mechanism for the following reaction?

(A) attack by CH_3O^-, then elimination of $CH_3CH_2CH_2O^-$
(B) elimination of $CH_3CH_2CH_2O^-$, then attack by CH_3O^-
(C) one-step backside attack by CH_3O^-
(D) through a carbonium ion intermediate

273. The following compound reacts with a hydrochloric acid solution.

What are the products of the reaction?

(A)

(B)

(C)

(D)

274. Which of the following compounds will most easily react with $H_2N(CH_2)_4NH_2$ to form a polymer?

(A)

$$Cl-\underset{\underset{O}{\|}}{C}-CH_2-\underset{\underset{O}{\|}}{C}-Cl$$

(B)

$$Cl-\underset{\underset{O}{\|}}{C}-CH_2-\underset{\underset{O}{\|}}{C}-H$$

(C)

$$CH_3-\underset{\underset{O}{\|}}{C}-CH_2-\underset{\underset{O}{\|}}{C}-Cl$$

(D)

$$Cl-\underset{\underset{O}{\|}}{C}-CH_2-\underset{\underset{O}{\|}}{C}-O-CH_3$$

275. An organic chemist produces the following compound by ozonolysis after an acid workup.

$$\underset{CH_3}{\overset{O}{\underset{\|}{C}}}\underset{CH_2}{}\underset{CH}{\overset{CH_3}{|}}\underset{CH_2}{}\underset{C}{\overset{O}{\underset{\|}{}}}CH_3$$

Which of the following compounds was the starting material?

(A)

$$\underset{CH_3}{\overset{OH}{\underset{|}{CH}}}\underset{CH_2}{}\underset{CH}{\overset{CH_3}{|}}\underset{CH_2}{}\underset{CH}{\overset{OH}{|}}CH_3$$

(B)

$$\begin{array}{c} CH_3 \\ \diagdown \\ \quad C = C \\ \diagup \quad \diagdown \\ CH \quad CH-CH_3 \\ \diagup \quad \diagup \\ CH_3 \quad CH_2 \end{array}$$

(C)

$$\underset{CH_3}{\overset{O}{\underset{\|}{C}}}\underset{CH_2}{}\underset{C}{\overset{CH_2}{\underset{\|}{}}}\underset{CH_2}{}\underset{C}{\overset{O}{\underset{\|}{}}}CH_3$$

(D)

$$\begin{array}{c} CH_3 \quad\quad CH_2 \\ \diagdown \quad\quad \diagup \\ \quad C \\ \| \quad\quad CH-CH_3 \\ \quad C \\ \diagup \quad\quad \diagdown \\ CH_3 \quad\quad CH_2 \end{array}$$

276. Which of the following compounds will NOT react with ethylamine to produce the following compound?

(A) benzaldehyde
(B) benzoyl chloride
(C) benzoic anhydride
(D) benzoic acid

277. What are the products of the reaction of isopropyl phenyl ether with hot concentrated hydrobromic acid?

(A) isopropyl bromide plus phenol
(B) isopropyl alcohol and phenol
(C) isopropyl alcohol plus bromobenzene
(D) isopropyl bromide plus bromobenzene

278. An organic chemistry student mixes the following chemicals.

$$\xrightarrow{\text{NaOH}}$$

Which of the following is the product of this reaction?

(A)

(B)

(C)

(D)

279. The following is part of the aldol condensation involving an enolate ion and an aldehyde

What is the role of the enolate ion?
(A) It is a nucleophile.
(B) It is an electrophile.
(C) It is a catalyst.
(D) It is a free radical.

280. The following reaction occurs upon heating. This step is an example of what type of reaction?

(A) addition
(B) elimination
(C) substitution
(D) dehydrogenation

281. An organic chemist is studying the following reaction.

1) NH_3
2) H^+/H_2O

During one experiment, he did not have sufficient NH_3. What would be the product of the first step if only one equivalent of NH_3 were available?

(A)

(B)

(C)

(D)

282. Which of the following reagents will serve to induce the following reaction?

(A) CrO_3
(B) $LiAlH_4$
(C) PBr_3
(D) H_3PO_4

283. The Barbier reaction involves the reaction of an alkyl halide with an aldehyde or ketone in the presence of a variety of reactants such as Mg, Li, or Zn. The generic reaction is

What type of reaction is this?
(A) Markovnikov addition
(B) oxidation
(C) nucleophilic substitution
(D) reduction

284. The peptide bonds in proteins are stabilized by resonance. Which of the following is LEAST effective in stabilizing the peptide bond?

(A)

(B)

(C)

(D)

285. The compound $C_{12}H_{14}O$ has a strong IR absorption near 1700 cm^{-1}. The treatment of the compound with excess EtMgBr followed by a workup using aqueous acid gave a new compound. Where would the new compound show a strong absorption in its IR spectrum?

(A) 3350 cm^{-1}
(B) 1700 cm^{-1}
(C) 3000 cm^{-1}
(D) 1650 cm^{-1}

286. The compound I has the formula $C_{22}H_{24}O$, and it has a strong IR absorption near 1700 cm^{-1}. The treatment of the compound with excess EtMgBr followed by a workup using aqueous acid gave a new compound, II. Treatment of compound II with acidic potassium dichromate gave compound III. Compound III had the formula $C_{24}H_{24}O_2$. Which of the three compounds could be extracted by aqueous sodium bicarbonate?

(A) I only
(B) II and III only
(C) III only
(D) I and II only

287. Traditionally, soaps are prepared from fats. Soaps contain the carboxylate ion of a fatty acid. The best way to produce a soap from a fat is to heat the fat with

(A) aqueous base
(B) aqueous acid
(C) chlorine
(D) potassium permanganate

288. What is the best reactant for producing benzyl acetate from benzyl alcohol?

(A) CH_3CH_2OH
(B) $(CH_3CO)_2O$
(C) CH_3COOH
(D) CH_3COCl

289. The acid-catalyzed reaction of ethanol with benzoic acid produces

(A) an ester
(B) another acid
(C) a ketal
(D) an ether

290. The reaction of chloroacetic acid with one equivalent of ammonia produces
   (A) $ClCH_2CONH_2$
   (B) H_2NCH_2COOH
   (C) $ClCH_2COO^-NH_4^+$
   (D) $H_2NCH_2COO^-$

291. The following is a simplified illustration of a Diels-Alder reaction

   During this reaction, there is a change in the number of σ bonds and π bonds. What is the overall change in each type of bond?
   (A) $+2$ σ and -2 π
   (B) -2 σ and $+2$ π
   (C) $+3$ σ and -3 π
   (D) -3 σ and $+3$ π

292. The saponification of an ester may produce the following products

   Which are the most likely products to form?
   (A) II and III
   (B) I and III
   (C) I and IV
   (D) II and IV

293. Which of the hydrogen atoms in the following compound is the most acidic?

(A) 4
(B) 3
(C) 2
(D) 1

294. Rank the following nitrophenols in order of increasing acidity.

I   II   III

(A) II < I < III
(B) I < II < III
(C) III < II < I
(D) II < III < I

295. Classify each of the following compounds as an acetal, a hemiacetal, or neither.

I II III

(A) I = neither, II = acetal, and III = hemiacetal
(B) I = acetal, II = hemiacetal, and III = neither
(C) I = hemiacetal, II = neither, and III = acetal
(D) I = acetal, II = neither, and III = hemiacetal

296. The experimental determination of the molar mass of acetic acid vapor results in a value of about 120 g/mol. What is the best explanation of this observation?

(A) Acetic acid undergoes an esterification reaction.
(B) Acetic acid undergoes a condensation reaction when it vaporizes.
(C) Acetic acid dehydrates to form acetic anhydride in the vapor phase.
(D) Acetic acid is present as hydrogen-bonded dimers.

297. The following nucleophile readily adds to the β-carbon because the π electrons are delocalized. The increased electron density is localized on which atom?

(A) the carbonyl oxygen
(B) the carbonyl carbon
(C) the γ-carbon
(D) the α-carbon

298. The following compound, benzoyl chloride, reacts with water to produce benzoic acid

This is an addition-elimination reaction where water

(A) and benzoyl chloride are nucleophiles, and the chloride ion is the electrophile

(B) is the electrophile, benzoyl chloride is the nucleophile, and the chloride ion is the leaving group

(C) and benzoyl chloride are electrophiles, and the chloride ion is the nucleophile

(D) is the nucleophile, benzoyl chloride is the electrophile, and the chloride ion is the leaving group

299. What is the major product of the reaction of excess propanal with hot aqueous base?

(A)

(B)

(C)

(D)

300. An organic chemist is investigating the following reaction.

$$\xrightarrow[\text{2) CH}_3\text{COOH}]{\text{1) NaOEt/EtOH}}$$

What is the major product of the reaction?

(A)

(B)

(C)

(D)

301. An organic chemist was investigating the following reaction.

What was the structure of the major product?

(A)

(B)

(C)

(D)

302. Which of the following is the most reactive?
  (A) acid chloride
  (B) acid anhydride
  (C) ether
  (D) ester

303. An organic chemist was investigating the following reaction of an alcohol with PCC (shown above the reaction arrow).

What was the structure of the major product?

(A)

(B)

(C)

(D)

304. Which of the following compounds is the strongest acid?

I   II   III

(A) III
(B) II
(C) I
(D) all equally strong

CHAPTER 6

Lab Technique and Spectroscopy

305. The incomplete reduction of an ester with sodium borohydride may yield an alcohol and boric acid. A chemist attempts to separate the products by extraction. The first step in the extraction is to treat the mixture with aqueous sodium bicarbonate and extract with ether. The next step is to treat the ether layer with sodium hydroxide. What product(s) will be in the ether layer after treatment?

    (A) alcohol only
    (B) alcohol and ester
    (C) boric acid
    (D) boric acid and alcohol

306. How many signals would appear in the ^{13}C NMR spectrum of the following compound?

    (A) 4
    (B) 6
    (C) 10
    (D) 12

307. How many ^{13}C NMR resonances appear in the spectrum of the following compound?

(A) 4
(B) 8
(C) 6
(D) 5

308. The monobromination of methylpropane gives predominantly one product. How many ^{1}H NMR signals does this product have?

(A) 1
(B) 4
(C) 3
(D) 2

309. Which of the following molecules contains only singlets in its proton NMR spectrum?

(A)

(B)

(C)

(D)

310. The following illustrates one method for synthesizing aspirin from salicylic acid and acetic acid.

Aspirin

The reaction does not go to completion. A researcher attempts to separate the mixture with aqueous sodium bicarbonate. Which of the components of the mixture will be in the aqueous layer?

(A) acetic acid and aspirin
(B) salicylic acid and acetic acid
(C) acetic acid only
(D) all three

311. When isopropyl alcohol is heated with sulfuric acid, two products may result. Depending upon the conditions, diisopropyl ether or propene may form. Which of the following observations in the IR spectrum would indicate that diisopropyl ether was the product?

(A) the absence of an O–H stretch
(B) the absence of a C=C stretch
(C) an increase in the intensity of the C–H stretch
(D) an increase in the band near 1700 cm^{-1}

312. An environmental chemist isolates a polluted sample believed to contain the following compounds.

I

II

III

IV

Extraction of the mixture with a sodium bicarbonate solution yielded an aqueous layer and an organic layer. Which of the compounds would be in the aqueous layer?

(A) II and IV
(B) I and III
(C) I and IV
(D) II and IV

313. How many ^1H NMR signals would be present in each of the following compounds?

I   II   III   IV

(A) I has 4, II has 2, III has 2, and IV has 1.
(B) I has 5, II has 4, III has 1, and IV has 2.
(C) I has 5, II has 2, III has 3, and IV has 2.
(D) I has 3, II has 2, III has 1, and IV has 1.

314. One reaction of alkenes is ozonolysis. The reaction sequence begins with the reaction with ozone and ends with a treatment of the ozonide formed with zinc and water. What is the characteristic IR peaks in every product?

    (A) 1300 cm^{-1}
    (B) 3300 cm^{-1}
    (C) 1700 cm^{-1}
    (D) 1250 cm^{-1}

315. Two compounds with the formula C_3H_7ClO are 1-chloro-2-methoxyethane and 1-chloro-2-propanol. Their boiling points are 93°C and 130°C, respectively. Why is the boiling point of 1-chloro-2-propanol higher?

    (A) It is capable of forming intermolecular hydrogen bonds.
    (B) Compounds with higher molecular weights have higher boiling points.
    (C) It is less polar than 1-chloro-2-methoxyethane.
    (D) It is more difficult to break all the bonds.

316. Which of the following compounds will exhibit a band in the 1700 cm^{-1} region of its IR spectrum?

    (A) $CH_3CH_2CH_2NH_2$
    (B) $CH_3CH_2C{\equiv}CH$
    (C) $CH_3CH_2CH_2OH$
    (D) $CH_3CH_2CH{=}O$

317. Which of the following laboratory techniques is NOT useful in the separation of a mixture of compounds?

    (A) extraction
    (B) chromatography
    (C) IR spectroscopy
    (D) distillation

318. Two compounds with the formula C_3H_7ClO are 1-chloro-2-methoxyethane and 1-chloro-2-propanol. Which of the following laboratory techniques would be the simplest method for separating a mixture of these two compounds?

    (A) extraction
    (B) distillation
    (C) thin layer chromatography
    (D) NMR spectroscopy

319. The chemical separation of a racemic mixture yields

    (A) separate enantiomers
    (B) another racemic mixture
    (C) separate diastereomers
    (D) a loss of optical activity

320. The separation of enantiomers is

    (A) crystallization
    (B) fractionation
    (C) resolution
    (D) distillation

321. The monochlorination of an alkane gave three products. Which of the following would be the BEST method for determining the structures of the products?

    (A) mass spec
    (B) NMR
    (C) IR
    (D) UV-Vis

322. Solvent extraction is a useful laboratory technique for separating mixtures. However, this method will not separate many combinations efficiently. A useful alternative to solvent extraction is

    (A) chromatography
    (B) IR spectroscopy
    (C) ultracentrifugation
    (D) filtration

323. The mononitration of toluene yields a mixture of 2-nitrotoluene and 4-nitrotoluene. The formula of both compounds is $C_7H_7NO_2$. Which of the following would be the best way to distinguish these compounds?

    (A) UV-Vis spectroscopy
    (B) mass spectroscopy
    (C) IR spectroscopy
    (D) NMR spectroscopy

324. The mononitration of toluene yields a mixture of 2-nitrotoluene and 4-nitrotoluene. The formula of both compounds is $C_7H_7NO_2$. Thin layer chromatography (TLC) was used to monitor the progress of this reaction. On a normal silica gel TLC plate, the unreacted toluene traveled farther. Which of the following best explains why toluene traveled farther than either of the nitro products?

    (A) Toluene has a lower molecular weight than nitrotoluene.
    (B) Toluene is polar, and nitrotoluene is nonpolar.
    (C) Toluene is nonpolar, and nitrotoluene is polar.
    (D) Toluene chemically reacts with the silica, and nitrotoluene does not.

325. The exhaustive nitration of benzene yields a compound with the formula $C_6H_3N_3O_6$. How many signals appear in the ^{13}C NMR spectrum of 1,3,5-trinitrobenzene?

(A) 2
(B) 6
(C) 1
(D) 3

326. A chemist isolates the following three compounds from a reaction mixture.

Which of the following would be the best way to differentiate these compounds?

(A) UV-Vis spectroscopy
(B) thin layer chromatography
(C) mass spectroscopy
(D) NMR spectroscopy

327. How many signals would appear in the ^1H NMR spectrum of the following compound?

(A) 2
(B) 3
(C) 5
(D) 6

328. Compound Y has the formula $C_{10}H_{16}O_2$. Compound Y reacts with lithium aluminum hydride to form Compound Z with the formula $C_{10}H_{20}O_2$. What might be the formula of the compound formed when Compound Z is heated with H_2SO_4?

(A) $C_{10}H_{16}$
(B) $C_{10}H_{16}O_3$
(C) $C_{10}H_{22}$
(D) $C_{10}H_8$

329. An IR absorption near 3400 cm^{-1} might indicate the presence of

(A) an aldehyde
(B) an alkene
(C) an alcohol
(D) a ketone

330. Which of the following compounds has three overlapping singlet peaks each integrating for three hydrogen atoms? (This may appear as one singlet integrating for nine hydrogen atoms.)

(A)

(B)

(C)

(D)

331. The addition of sodium hydroxide to 1-bromopentane yields sodium bromide and 1-pentanol. Which of the two organic compounds (1-bromopentane or 1-pentanol) has the higher boiling point?

(A) 1-pentanol because of hydrogen bonding
(B) 1-bromopentane because of higher molecular weight
(C) 1-pentanol because of polymerization
(D) 1-bromopentane because it has a greater dipole moment

332. Which spectroscopic method affects the electronic structure of the molecule being studied?

(A) ultraviolet-visible spectroscopy
(B) infrared spectroscopy
(C) mass spectroscopy
(D) NMR spectroscopy

333. An unknown compound has a strong IR absorption near 1700 cm^{-1}. The proton NMR had no signal in the 9–10 ppm region and gave a negative Tollens' test. Iodoform forms when the compound reacts with a mixture of I$_2$/NaOH. Which of the following might the unknown compound be?

(A)

(B)

(C)

(D)

334. Sulfonation of toluene will yield both ortho and para toluenesulfonic acid. In order to monitor the progress of the reaction, an organic chemist periodically removes a sample from the reaction mixture and places it on a normal silica gel TLC (thin layer chromatography) plate. Which of the following is true?

(A) Toluene travels farther because it is less polar than toluenesulfonic acid.
(B) Toluene travels farther because it is more polar than toluenesulfonic acid.
(C) Toluenesulfonic acid travels farther because it is less polar than toluene.
(D) Toluenesulfonic acid travels farther because it is more polar than toluene.

335. The reduction of an ester with sodium borohydride can produce an alcohol and boric acid. A chemist attempts to separate the products by extraction. The first step in the extraction is to treat the mixture with aqueous sodium bicarbonate and extract with ether. What product(s) will be in the aqueous layer after treatment?

(A) boric acid only
(B) ester only
(C) boric acid and ester
(D) all three products

336. How many ^{13}C resonances will appear in the NMR of the following compound?

(A) 10
(B) 8
(C) 12
(D) 14

337. The ^{1}H NMR spectrum of an organic compound showed, among other things, a triplet integrating for nine hydrogen atoms. How many hydrogen atoms are adjacent to the hydrogen atoms giving rise to this triplet?

(A) 1
(B) 2
(C) 3
(D) 9

338. The compound C_5H_8O has an IR band at 1715 cm^{-1}. What functional group is indicated?

(A) a carboxylic acid
(B) an ester
(C) a ketone
(D) an alcohol

339. Which of the following proton NMR signals represents the most deshielded proton?

(A) 7.2 ppm
(B) 9.8 ppm
(C) 2.5 ppm
(D) 1.5 ppm

340. The ^{1}H NMR of ketone shows five signals. Reduction of this compound with sodium borohydride and treating the product with acid followed by aqueous workup yields a new compound. How many new signals will be in the ^{1}H NMR of the new compound?

(A) 0
(B) 1
(C) 2
(D) 3

341. The major peaks in the IR spectrum of a compound are at 2990, 1715, 1640, and 915 cm^{-1}. Which functional group is NOT present?

(A) alcohol
(B) ester
(C) aldehyde
(D) ketone

342. The Kuhn-Winterstein reaction converts 1,2-glycols to trans-alkenes using a variety of reagents such as P_2I_4. The generic reaction is

What is the easiest method of separating large amounts of the product from unreacted starting material?

(A) electrophoresis
(B) extraction into aqueous base
(C) thin layer chromatography
(D) distillation

343. The Leuckart reaction involves the reaction of aldehydes or ketones with ammonium salts of formic acid. The general reaction is

$$\underset{R}{\overset{O}{\|}}\underset{R}{\overset{}{\bigwedge}} \quad + \quad NH_4^+CHO_2^- \quad \xrightarrow{\Delta} \quad \xrightarrow{H^+} \quad \underset{R}{\overset{NH_2}{\bigwedge}}\underset{R}{}$$

What is the easiest method of separating the product from unreacted starting material?

(A) First extract with water; then extract with acid.
(B) First extract with water, then extract with base.
(C) First extract with ether, then extract with alcohol.
(D) First extract with ether, then extract with base.

344. It is possible to separate amino acids by electrophoresis. During electro-phoresis, an applied electric field separates the molecules. Every amino acid has at least two pK_a values, one for the carboxylic acid group and one for the amino group. Some amino acids have an additional pK_a value for the side chain. For alanine, the pK_a values are 2.3 and 9.6 (carboxylic acid and amino groups, respectively). Which of the following is true concerning an electrophoresis experiment?

(A) In a 0.1 M NaOH solution, alanine will migrate toward the positive plate.

(B) In a 0.1 M NaOH solution, alanine will migrate toward the negative plate.

(C) In a 0.1 M HCl solution, alanine will migrate toward the positive plate.

(D) In a 0.1 M HCl solution, alanine will not migrate toward either plate.

345. A chemist extracts several compounds from a plant into ether. Through a series of extractions, she isolates a mixture of two compounds. Separation of the two compounds on a TLC plate showed compound I to have an R_f value of 0.3 and compound II to have an R_f value of 0.8. What do the R_f values indicate?

(A) Compound II is more polar than compound I.

(B) Compound I is more polar than compound II.

(C) Compound I has a higher molecular weight than compound II.

(D) Compound II has a higher molecular weight than compound I.

346. Compound I has the formula $C_{12}H_{18}O_2$ and shows an IR absorption at 1740 cm^{-1}. Treatment of the compound with aqueous HCl and heat resulted in another compound, II, with an IR absorption at 1710 cm^{-1}. What type of functional group was present in compound I?

(A) ketone

(B) ether

(C) carboxylic acid

(D) ester

347. A compound X reacts with a mixture of I_2 in aqueous NaOH to form an odiferous yellow precipitate. What type of compound could compound X be?

(A) a methyl ketone

(B) an alcohol

(C) an ether

(D) a carboxylic acid

348. Compound Y has the formula $C_{10}H_{16}O_2$. Compound Y reacts with lithium aluminum hydride to form compound Z with the formula $C_{10}H_{20}O_2$. How many rings could compound Y have?

(A) 4
(B) 3
(C) 2
(D) 1

349. Benzoyl peroxide is useful in the formation of polymers such as polymethylmethacrylate (Lucite). This compound initiates polymerization following the homolytic cleavage of the O–O bond. What type of step is this?

(A) an initiation step
(B) a propagation step
(C) an instigation step
(D) a proliferation step

350. How many resonances would appear in the ^{13}C NMR of the following compound?

(A) 4
(B) 3
(C) 8
(D) 2

351. Which of the following compounds exhibit spin-spin coupling in their proton NMR?

(A) CH_3Cl
(B) $HOCH_2CH_2OH$
(C) $CH_3CH_2CH_2Cl$
(D) $CH_2=C=O$

352. Which of the following compounds will exhibit a band in the 2100 cm^{-1} region of their IR spectrum?

(A) $CH_3CH_2CH=O$
(B) $CH_3CH_2C\equiv CH$
(C) $CH_3CH_2CH_2OH$
(D) $CH_3CH_2CH_2NH_2$

353. What is the best treatment to extract an amine into an aqueous phase from a mixture?

(A) Use 0.1 M HCl.
(B) Use 0.1 M NaHCO$_3$.
(C) Use 0.1 M NaOH.
(D) Use 0.1 M C$_2$H$_5$OH.

354. The monobromination of isobutane produces one major product. The number of proton NMR signals of the product would be

(A) a singlet and a multiplet
(B) a singlet
(C) a doublet
(D) a triplet and a quartet

355. Which of the following would be the best method for separating 1-hexanol from dipropyl ether?

(A) filtration
(B) extraction with base
(C) extraction with acid
(D) fractional distillation

356. What splitting pattern is expected for the indicated methyl group in the following compound?

(A) singlet
(B) doublet
(C) triplet
(D) multiplet

357. A compound with the formula C$_4$H$_8$ shows only one peak in its NMR spectrum. What is the compound?

(A) 2-butene
(B) methylpropene
(C) 1-butene
(D) cyclobutane

358. How many ^{13}C NMR signals would be present in each of the following compounds?

I   II   III   IV

(A) I has 2, II has 4, III has 4, and IV has 1.
(B) I has 6, II has 4, III has 2, and IV has 2.
(C) I has 4, II has 3, III has 4, and IV has 2.
(D) I has 2, II has 6, III has 3, and IV has 1.

359. An organic chemist investigates the following reaction.

$$\xrightarrow[\text{H}_2\text{SO}_4]{\text{K}_2\text{Cr}_2\text{O}_7}$$

Which of the following observations in the IR spectrum would indicate that the reaction went to completion?

(A) the disappearance of the C–C stretch
(B) the appearance of the C=O stretch
(C) the disappearance of the O–H stretch
(D) the appearance of the C=C stretch

360. An environmental chemist isolates a polluted sample believed to contain the following compounds.

I   II

III   IV

Extraction of the mixture with dilute HCl yielded an aqueous layer and an organic layer. Which of the compounds would be in the aqueous layer?

(A) III, I, and II
(B) II and IV
(C) IV
(D) III

361. The monobromination of 2-methylbutane can yield a number of products. What would be the most efficient method of separating a 100 mL mixture of the isomers?

(A) fractional distillation
(B) solvent extraction
(C) paper chromatography
(D) titration

362. The following illustrates one method for synthesizing aspirin from salicylic acid and acetic acid.

Aspirin

Which of the compounds will show a strong absorption near 1700 cm^{-1} in the IR spectrum?

(A) aspirin only
(B) salicylic acid and acetic acid
(C) acetic acid only
(D) all three

363. Epoxides react via an S$_N$2 mechanism with methyl sulfide ions. The following is a typical example.

It would be possible to monitor the progress of this reaction by removing samples, neutralizing, extracting to separate the material from water, and then examining changes in which region of the IR spectrum?

(A) 1700 cm^{-1}
(B) 3000 cm^{-1}
(C) 3600 cm^{-1}
(D) 1000 cm^{-1}

364. The free radical monochlorination of 2-methylbutane will give the following products.

Which of the following methods would be the best at identifying the different products?

(A) ^{1}H NMR spectroscopy
(B) IR spectroscopy
(C) mass spectroscopy
(D) UV-Vis spectroscopy

365. How many ^{1}H NMR resonances appear in the aromatic region of the following ion?

(A) 0
(B) 3
(C) 5
(D) 4

366. It is possible to separate amino acids by electrophoresis. During electrophoresis, an applied electric field separates the molecules. Every amino acid has at least two pK$_a$ values, one for the carboxylic acid group and one for the amino group. Some amino acids have an additional pK$_a$ value for the side chain. For asparagine, the pK$_a$ values are 2.0 and 8.8 (carboxylic acid and amino groups, respectively). The pI value for an amino acid is the average of the pK$_a$ values. At a pH = pI, the carboxylic acid group is deprotonated and the amino group is protonated. Which of the following is true concerning an electrophoresis experiment?

(A) At pH = 5.4, asparagine will not migrate toward either plate.
(B) At pH = 5.4, asparagine will migrate toward the positive plate.
(C) At pH = 1.0, asparagine will migrate toward the positive plate.
(D) At pH = 11.0, asparagine will migrate toward the negative plate.

CHAPTER 7

Bioorganic Chemistry

367. Treatment of an octapeptide with 2,4-dinitrofluorobenzene followed by hydrolysis gave only residues with the dinitrophenyl group attached to glycine. The reaction mechanism leading to the attachment of the 2,4-dinitrofluorobenzene is

(A) nucleophilic aromatic substitution
(B) electrophilic aromatic substitution
(C) S_N1
(D) E2

368. This is the structure of nicotine.

What is the absolute configuration of nicotine?

(A) R
(B) S
(C) achiral
(D) impossible to determine

369. The generic formula for an amino acid is

$$H_2N—C(H)(R)—C(=O)(OH)$$

Why are amino acids considered to be amphoteric?

(A) They have both D and L forms.
(B) They may undergo oxidation or reduction.
(C) They may behave as an acid or as a base.
(D) They can form enantiomers.

370. Maltose is a disaccharide formed by joining two glucose molecules by a glycoside linkage. The structure of maltose is

Which of the following best describes the glycoside linkage?

(A) α-1,4
(B) β-1,4
(C) α-1,2
(D) β-1,2

371. The disaccharide lactose has the following structure.

Which of the following is NOT true about lactose?

(A) It has a hemiacetal.
(B) It has more than 100 stereoisomers.
(C) It is a dipeptide.
(D) It has a glycoside linkage.

372. The structure of testosterone is

How many stereoisomers of testosterone are possible?

(A) 6
(B) 24
(C) 32
(D) 64

373. Referring to the structure of testosterone, pictured in the previous question, what is its degree of unsaturation?

(A) 4
(B) 6
(C) 2
(D) 8

374. Physiological pH is 7.4. What does this mean?

(A) It is slightly more basic than pure water.
(B) It is slightly more acidic than pure water.
(C) The concentration of H⁺ is less than the concentration of OH⁻.
(D) both A and C

375. The pI of the amino acid leucine is 5.98. A sample of leucine is placed in a solution buffered at a pH of 5.98. Then two electrodes are placed into the solution and connected to a battery. Toward which electrode will the majority of the leucine migrate?

(A) toward the negative electrode
(B) toward the positive electrode
(C) toward neither electrode
(D) half toward each electrode

376. Which of the following sugars are aldopentoses?

(A) I and III
(B) I, III, and IV
(C) I, II, and III
(D) II and IV

377. Pentoses and hexoses may form cyclic structures with five or six atoms in the ring. Why do they not form cyclic structures with smaller ring sizes?

(A) Smaller rings rapidly polymerize to form polysaccharides.
(B) Smaller rings require unstable angles that are greater than tetrahedral.
(C) Smaller rings rapidly react to form disaccharides.
(D) Smaller rings require unstable angles that are less than tetrahedral.

378. The tertiary structure of proteins normally places the polar side chains
    (A) in the active site
    (B) in position to react with each other
    (C) on the exterior of the protein
    (D) on the interior of the protein

379. What type of compound is the phosphate ester of a nucleoside?
    (A) DNA
    (B) nucleotide
    (C) pyramidine
    (D) RNA

380. Many organic functional groups are important in biological systems. For example, fats contain ester groups and proteins contain amide groups. In the laboratory, both acid chlorides and acid anhydrides are useful in the synthesis of these functional groups. However, neither acid chlorides nor acid anhydrides are important in the biosynthesis of esters or amides. These compounds are NOT important in biological systems because they
    (A) are too reactive to exist in biological systems
    (B) are nonpolar and are not soluble in biological (aqueous) systems
    (C) only react at higher temperatures than are present in biological systems
    (D) are less efficient than the enzymes present in biological systems

381. Saponification is the base-catalyzed hydrolysis of an ester. The saponification of a fat produces glycerol and the carboxylate salt of the base. The carboxylate portion typically has 10 to 20 carbon atoms. In aqueous solution, the carboxylate salt exists in a structure known as a micelle. The structure of a micelle is a conglomerate with the
    (A) hydrophilic carboxylate groups on the exterior and the hydrophobic hydrocarbon portions on the interior
    (B) hydrophobic carboxylate groups on the exterior and the hydrophilic hydrocarbon portions on the interior
    (C) hydrophilic carboxylate groups on the interior and the hydrophobic hydrocarbon portions on the exterior
    (D) hydrophobic carboxylate groups on the interior and the hydrophilic hydrocarbon portions on the exterior

382. One of the many methods for synthesizing amino acids in the laboratory is the Strecker synthesis. In one experiment, an organic chemist utilized the method to prepare an amino acid. The compound she isolated was not optically active. Which of the following is the isolated amino acid ?
    (A) alanine
    (B) proline
    (C) glycine
    (D) lysine

383. The structure of the amino acid ornithine is

$$H_2N - CH - \overset{\displaystyle \overset{O}{\|}}{C} - OH$$

with the side chain:

CH$_2$
CH$_2$
CH$_2$
NH$_2$

How does the isoelectric point of alanine compare to that of ornithine?

(A) Alanine has a higher value.
(B) Alanine has a lower value.
(C) Alanine has about the same value.
(D) It is not possible to determine from the information given.

384. It is possible to synthesize an amino acid from an aldehyde through the Strecker synthesis. The general method for synthesizing an amino acid is

What is the role of the ammonia?

(A) It is a nucleophile.
(B) It is an electrophile.
(C) It is an acid.
(D) It is a catalyst.

385. The structures of the amino acids serine and lysine are

Serine

Lysine

Which of the following statements is true?

(A) Serine has two pK_a values, and lysine has two K_a values.
(B) Serine has three pK_a values, and lysine has three K_a values.
(C) Serine has one pK_a value, and lysine has two K_a values.
(D) Serine has two pK_a values, and lysine has three K_a values.

The next five questions refer to the following figure.

This carbohydrate sequence represents the terminal sequence of the Type A determinant protein in blood.

386. Which unit will give a positive Benedict's test as a reducing sugar?

(A) none
(B) unit A
(C) unit C
(D) unit D

387. What are the forms of the anomeric carbon atoms in units A and D?

(A) A is an acetal, and D is a hemiacetal.
(B) A is a hemiacetal, and D is an acetal.
(C) A is a hemiacetal, and D is a hemiacetal.
(D) A is an acetal, and D is an acetal.

388. How many degrees of unsaturation are present in this carbohydrate sequence?

(A) 8
(B) 4
(C) 9
(D) 6

389. Which unit is a maltose unit?

(A) A
(B) B
(C) D
(D) none

390. What is the best description of the linkage between unit D and unit B?

(A) β-1,3
(B) β-1,2
(C) α-1,2
(D) α-1,3

The next two questions refer to the following situation.

The partial hydrolysis of a hexapeptide yielded the following dipeptide fragments:

gly-ala   ser-gly   ser-pro   ala-ser   gly-ser

The following tripeptides were also found:

gly-ala-ser   gly-ser-pro   ala-ser-gly

Analysis of the hexapeptide found it to contain 1 ala residue, 2 gly residues, 1 pro residue, and 2 ser residues. Treatment of the hexapeptide with 2,4-dinitrofluorobenzene followed by hydrolysis gave only residues with the dinitrophenyl group attached to glycine.

391. This information indicates that 2,4-dinitrofluorobenzene is useful in protein analysis because

(A) It is the most abundant amino acid in the protein.
(B) It attaches to the C-terminal amino acid.
(C) It attaches to the N-terminal amino acid.
(D) It is the most reactive amino acid in the protein.

392. What is the amino acid sequence?

(A) gly-ala-ser-gly-ser-pro
(B) gly-ser-pro-gly-ala-ser
(C) ala-ser-gly-gly-ser-pro
(D) pro-ser-gly-ser-ala-gly

393. The most commonly used conditions for the complete hydrolysis of a protein are

(A) hot concentrated base
(B) hot concentrated acid
(C) room temperature dilute acid
(D) room temperature dilute base

394. Alitame is an artificial sweetener with the following structure.

Alitame is more stable than aspartame and about 2,000 times as sweet as sucrose. The most basic group in alitame is

(A) the amino group
(B) both the amide nitrogen atoms
(C) the sulfur
(D) the carbonyl oxygen atoms

395. Para-aminosalicyclic acid is a secondary line drug for the treatment of tuberculosis. The structure of para-aminosalicyclic acid is

What is the form of this drug at pH = 14?

(A)

(B)

(C)

(D)

396. Reduction of the aldehyde group of the carbohydrate D-allose yields allitol. The structure of allitol is

Allitol is a

(A) chiral compound
(B) carbohydrate
(C) meso compound
(D) polymeric compound

397. Referring to the figure in question 396, what type of compound would form if the alcohol group on the second carbon atom underwent oxidation?

(A) a ketohexose
(B) an aldohexose
(C) an acidic alcohol
(D) a carboxylic acid

398. Which of the following configurations may be present in naturally occurring carbohydrates?

I α   II β   III D   IV L

(A) I and III
(B) I, II, and III
(C) I, II, and IV
(D) I, II, III, and IV

399. This is the structure of the amino acid isoleucine.

$$
\begin{array}{c}
\overset{\displaystyle O}{\underset{\displaystyle \parallel}{}} \\
H_2N-CH-C-OH \\
| \\
CH-CH_3 \\
| \\
CH_2 \\
| \\
CH_3
\end{array}
$$

Which of the following is the zwitterion form of isoleucine?

(A)
$$
\begin{array}{c}
O \\
\parallel \\
H_2N-CH-C-OH \\
| \\
CH-CH_3 \\
| \\
CH_2 \\
| \\
CH_3
\end{array}
$$

(B)
$$
\begin{array}{c}
O \\
\parallel \\
H_2N-CH-C-\overset{\ominus}{O} \\
| \\
CH-CH_3 \\
| \\
CH_2 \\
| \\
CH_3
\end{array}
$$

(C)
$$
\begin{array}{c}
\quad\quad\quad O \\
\overset{\oplus}{} \quad\quad \parallel \\
H_3N-CH-C-OH \\
| \\
CH-CH_3 \\
| \\
CH_2 \\
| \\
CH_3
\end{array}
$$

(D)
$$
\begin{array}{c}
\quad\quad\quad O \\
\overset{\oplus}{} \quad\quad \parallel \\
H_3N-CH-C-\overset{\ominus}{O} \\
| \\
CH-CH_3 \\
| \\
CH_2 \\
| \\
CH_3
\end{array}
$$

400. Which of the following Fischer projections represents an L-monosaccharide?

(A)

(B)

(C)

(D)

401. Alitame is an artificial sweetener with the following structure.

Alitame is more stable than aspartame and about 2,000 times as sweet as sucrose. Which of the following is true about alitame in the stomach (pH = 1)?

(A) The amino group would be protonated.
(B) The amide nitrogen atoms would be protonated.
(C) All the nitrogen atoms would be protonated.
(D) The overall charge would be 0.

402. Most amino acids are chiral compounds. Which of the following amino acids is achiral?

(A)

$$H_2N-CH-\overset{\overset{\displaystyle O}{\|}}{C}-OH$$

$$\underset{\underset{\displaystyle SH}{|}}{\overset{|}{CH_2}}$$

(B) $H_2N-CH-\overset{\overset{\displaystyle O}{\|}}{C}-OH$

$\overset{|}{H}$

(C)

$$H_2N-CH-\overset{\overset{\displaystyle O}{\|}}{C}-OH$$

$$\underset{\underset{\displaystyle CH_3}{|}}{\overset{|}{CH}-OH}$$

(D)

$\overset{\overset{\displaystyle O}{\|}}{C}-OH$

HN

403. The following presents two representations of D-gulose. Which position in the right-hand structure is the same as the circled alcohol group in the left-hand structure?

(A) 6
(B) 4
(C) 3
(D) 2

404. An amino acid is at its isoelectric point. Decreasing the hydrogen ion concentration will cause what change in the overall charge?

(A) neutral to positive
(B) neutral to negative
(C) positive to negative
(D) negative to positive

405. Which of the following amino acids would most likely be in a nonpolar region of a protein?

(A)

$$H_2N-CH-C-OH$$

with O double bonded to C, and CH connected to CH_2 connected to a benzene ring

(B)

$$H_2N-CH-C-OH$$

with O double bonded to C, and CH connected to CH_2 connected to SH

(C)

$$H_2N-CH-C-OH$$

with O double bonded to C, and CH connected to $CH-OH$ connected to CH_3

(D)

$$H_2N-CH-C-OH$$

with O double bonded to C, and CH connected to CH_2 connected to OH

406. The drug thalidomide was introduced in the late 1950s to alleviate the morning sickness that often accompanies pregnancy. Synthesis of the drug resulted in a racemic mixture. One of the enantiomers was the active ingredient for treating morning sickness, while the other enantiomer led to birth defects. The following is one of the enantiomers of thalidomide. What is the most likely explanation of why the two forms of thalidomide have different activities?

(A) the interaction with a receptor or enzyme
(B) the ability to transport into the cells
(C) the greater solubility of one form
(D) the greater polarity of one form

407. Which of the following would be an example of an α-amino acid?

(A)

(B)

(C) $H_2N—CH—\overset{\overset{\displaystyle O}{\|}}{C}—NH_2$

$\quad\quad\quad\quad CH_3$

(D)

$H_2N—CH—\overset{\overset{\displaystyle O}{\|}}{C}—OMe$

$\quad\quad\quad CH_2$

$\quad\quad\quad SH$

408. Alitame is an artificial sweetener with the following structure.

Alitame is more stable than aspartame and about 2,000 times as sweet as sucrose. The ^1H NMR of the methyl group attached to the chiral carbon would show

(A) a singlet
(B) a triplet
(C) a doublet
(D) a quartet

409. The structure of the amino acid ornithine is

$$H_2N-CH-\overset{\overset{\displaystyle O}{\|}}{C}-OH$$

$$\underset{\underset{\underset{\underset{\displaystyle NH_2}{|}}{\displaystyle CH_2}}{\diagup}}{\overset{\displaystyle |}{CH_2}}\overset{\diagdown}{CH_2}$$

At what pH is this the predominant form of ornithine?

(A) It is stable near a neutral pH.
(B) It is stable at low pHs.
(C) It is stable at high pHs.
(D) It is never the predominant form.

410. Homoserine is not a common amino acid, but it is important in the bio-synthesis of methionine, threonine, and isoleucine. Which of the following is the best representation of the zwitterionic form of homoserine?

(A)

$$H_2N-CH-C(=O)-OH$$
$$|$$
$$CH_2$$
$$|$$
$$CH_2$$
$$|$$
$$OH$$

(B)

$$\overset{\oplus}{H_3N}-CH-C(=O)-OH$$
$$|$$
$$CH_2$$
$$|$$
$$CH_2$$
$$|$$
$$OH$$

(C)

$$H_2N-CH-C(=O)-\overset{\ominus}{O}$$
$$|$$
$$CH_2$$
$$|$$
$$CH_2$$
$$|$$
$$OH$$

(D)

$$\overset{\oplus}{H_3N}-CH-C(=O)-\overset{\ominus}{O}$$
$$|$$
$$CH_2$$
$$|$$
$$CH_2$$
$$|$$
$$OH$$

411. The amino acid valine has a $pK_a = 2.3$ for the carboxyl end and a $pK_a = 9.6$ for the amino end. This means the pI for valine is 5.95 (the average of the two pK_a values). Which of the following is true concerning a 1 mM valine solution buffered at pH 2.3?

(A) There are equal concentrations of the zwitterion form and the form with a +1 net charge.

(B) There are equal concentrations of the zwitterion form and the form with a −1 net charge.

(C) Only the fully protonated form is present.

(D) Only the fully deprotonated form is present.

412. The amino acid valine has a $pK_a = 2.3$ for the carboxyl end and a $pK_a = 9.6$ for the amino end. This means the pI for valine is 5.95 (the average of the two pK_a values). Which of the following is true concerning a 1 mM valine solution buffered at pH 12?

(A)

(B)

(C)

(D)

413. Enzymes known as α-glucosidases catalyze the hydrolysis of carbohydrates to monosaccharides. Two of these enzymes are sucrase and maltase. These enzymes hydrolyze sucrose and maltose, respectively. The action of these enzymes produces which of the following monosaccharides?

(A) glucose and fructose
(B) glucose and sorbose
(C) sorbose and fructose
(D) glucose only

414. Examine the following two carbohydrates:

Which of the following terms would be useful in describing the relationship between these molecules?

    I.   epimers
    II. anomers
    III. diastereomers

(A) I, II, and III
(B) I and II
(C) II only
(D) I only

415. The compound miglitol is an inhibitor of α-glucosidases. The structure of miglitol is

The absolute configurations about carbon atoms 2 and 5 are

(A) 2S and 5R
(B) 2R and 5R
(C) 2S and 5S
(D) 2R and 5S

416. The following reaction, accompanied by ATP and appropriate enzymes, occurs in biological systems.

The bond formed during this process is

(A) an ether
(B) an acid anhydride
(C) an ester
(D) a phosphine

417. Epimerase is an enzyme that can catalyze the isomerization of D-ribulose 5-phosphate to D-xylulose 5-phosphate. Which of the following is NOT an isomerization reaction?

(A) $CH_3CH_2COCl + H_2O \rightarrow HCl + CH_3CH_2COOH$
(B) trans-$CH_3CH=CHCH_3$ → cis-$CH_3CH=CHCH_3$
(C) $CH_3CH_2C(CH_3)_3$ → $(CH_3)_2CHCH(CH_3)_2$
(D) $CH_3CH_2CHOHCHOHCH_3$ → $CH_3CH_2C(OH)_2CH_2CH_3$

418. Which of the following is true concerning the classification of monosaccharides with six carbon atoms?

(A) D-glucose and D-fructose have the same number of stereoisomers.
(B) Each D-aldose has two anomers.
(C) D-glucose has 32 stereoisomers.
(D) Aldoses and hexoses have the same number of stereoisomers.

419. Polyunsaturated fats have lower melting points than saturated fats of comparable size. The unsaturation in most natural polyunsaturated fats is due to carbon-carbon double bonds, which are present exclusively as the cis isomer. Industrially, the partial hydrogenation of a polyunsaturated fat is a useful technique to increase the melting point and yield a commercial product. What conditions are necessary for partial hydrogenation of a fat?

(A) $LiAlH_4/Et_2O$
(B) H^+/H_2O
(C) H_2/Ni
(D) H_2/Δ

420. The formation of hydrogen bonds between the peptide bonds of a protein leads to the

(A) primary structure
(B) secondary structure
(C) tertiary structure
(D) quaternary structure

421. Peptide bonds hold the amino acids in a protein together. What is another name for a peptide bond?

(A) hydrogen bond
(B) glycoside linkage
(C) ester bond
(D) amide bond

422. Polyunsaturated fats have lower melting points than saturated fats of comparable size. The unsaturation in most natural polyunsaturated fats is due to carbon-carbon double bonds, which are present exclusively as the cis isomer. Industrially, the partial hydrogenation of a polyunsaturated fat is a useful technique to increase the melting point and yield a commercial product. The increase in the melting point is a result of increased

(A) hydrogen bonding between the straighter chains
(B) London dispersion forces between the straighter chains
(C) London dispersion forces due to isomerization of the double bonds
(D) hydrogen bonding due to isomerization of the double bonds

423. Lactic acid has a pK_a of 3.85. What is the ratio of lactate ion to lactic acid in a solution at pH = 3.85?

(A) 1.00
(B) 3.85
(C) > 3.85
(D) 7.00

424. The zwitterion form of an amino acid is the predominant species in solution when the pH of the solution equals the pI of the amino acid. The pK_a of the carboxylic acid of alanine is 2.35, and the pK_a of the ammonium form of the amino group is 9.69. What is the pI value of alanine?

(A) 7.00
(B) 6.02
(C) 2.35
(D) 9.69

425. Acid hydrolysis of a tripeptide yielded equal amounts of each of the following three amino acids: leu, cys, and ala. What was the probable order of the amino acids in the tripeptide?

(A) ala-leu-cys
(B) leu-cys-ala
(C) leu-ala-cys
(D) It is impossible to determine.

426. Two molecules of the amino acid cysteine can join to form cysteine. The reaction is

What type of reaction is this?

(A) oxidation-reduction
(B) neutralization
(C) decomposition
(D) polymerization

427. Glucose is a reducing sugar, which means that it will give a positive Benedict's test. A positive Benedict's test is the formation of a red precipitate of Cu_2O, which forms as the sugar undergoes oxidation by Cu^{2+}. The following equilibrium is present in all glucose solutions.

The ring forms will not give a positive Benedict's test. In one solution, 43% of the glucose is in the "straight" chain form. What percent of the glucose in this solution will react to give a positive Benedict's test?

(A) 0%
(B) 43%
(C) 57%
(D) 100%

428. This is the structure of adenine.

Which of the following is an acceptable resonance form for adenine?

(A)

(B)

(C)

(D)

429. The drug thalidomide was introduced in the late 1950s to alleviate the morning sickness that often accompanies pregnancy. Synthesis of the drug resulted in a racemic mixture. One of the enantiomers was the active ingredient for treating morning sickness, while the other enantiomer led to birth defects. The following is one of the enantiomers of thalidomide. What are the expected hybridizations of the two nitrogen atoms in thalidomide?

(A) N-1 is sp^3, and N-2 is sp^2.
(B) N-1 is sp, and N-2 is sp^2.
(C) N-1 is sp^2, and N-2 is sp^3.
(D) N-1 is sp^3, and N-2 is sp^3.

CHAPTER 8

Final Review

430. Esters will undergo both acid-catalyzed and base-catalyzed hydrolysis. However, there is a difference in the products. What is this difference?

(A) Acid catalysis produces the carboxylic acid and the alcohol, while base catalysis produces the carboxylate ion and the alcohol.

(B) Base catalysis produces the carboxylic acid and the alcohol, while acid catalysis produces the carboxylate ion and the alcohol.

(C) Acid catalysis produces the carboxylic acid and the alcohol, while base catalysis produces the carboxylate ion and the alkoxide ion.

(D) Acid catalysis produces the carboxylic acid and the dehydration product of the alcohol, while base catalysis produces the carboxylate ion and the alcohol.

431. Which of the following is an acid anhydride?

(A)

(B)

(C)

(D)

432. Chymostatin is a drug used to interfere with the action of the enzyme chymotrypsin. The drug preferentially binds to the active site of chymotrypsin to reduce its activity. What type of interaction is this?

(A) competitive inhibition
(B) noncompetitive inhibition
(C) negative feedback
(D) nucleophilic attack

433. What is the product of the reaction of CD_3OH with isopropylmagnesium bromide?

(A)

$$CD_3 - O - \underset{\underset{CH_3}{|}}{\overset{\overset{CH_3}{|}}{CH}}$$

(B)

$$CH_3 - \underset{\underset{OH}{|}}{CH} - CH_3$$

(C)

$$CH_3 - \underset{\underset{OD}{|}}{CH} - CH_3$$

(D) $CH_3 - CH_2 - CH_3$

434. For $CH_3CH_2CHOHCH_2CH_3$ and $CH_3CH_2CDOHCH_2CH_3$ it is possible to oxidize them with acidic $K_2Cr_2O_7$. How do the two rates of reaction compare?

(A) The deuterated form reacts slower.
(B) The deuterated form reacts faster.
(C) The two forms react at the same rate.
(D) It is not possible to predict the relative rates.

435. Which of the following compounds will extract into sodium bicarbonate, but not into ether or dilute hydrochloric acid?

(A)

NH_2

(B)

OH

(C)

OH (with C=O)

(D)

NH_2 (with C=O)

436. What is the major product of the reaction of (R)-2-bromopentane with excess hydroxide ion?

(A) (S)-2-pentanol
(B) (R)-2-pentanol
(C) racemic 2-pentanol
(D) 2-bromo-1-pentanol

437. Which of the following compounds would undergo the fastest dehydration when treated with concentrated phosphoric acid?

(A) OH

(B) OH

(C) OH

(D) OH

438. A polymer has the following structure.

$$(-CH_2-CCl=CCl-CH_2-)_n$$

What is the structure of the monomer?

(A) $CH_2=CHCl-CHCl=CH_2$
(B) $CH_3CCl=CCl-CH_3$
(C) $CH_2=CHCl$
(D) $CH_2=CHCl$ plus $CH_2=CH_2$

439. Which of the following is NOT true concerning cyclohexyllithium?

(A) It is a strong oxidizing agent.
(B) It reacts with water to form cyclohexane.
(C) It is a weak reducing agent.
(D) It is formed when cyclohexyl bromide reacts with lithium metal.

440. A scientist wishes to prepare the following molecule by reaction with bromine.

What was the other reactant?

(A) trans-3-hexene
(B) cis-3-hexene
(C) 2,3-hexadiene
(D) 2-hexene

441. Which of the following is a correct Lewis structure for one of the resonance forms of the bicarbonate ion?

(A)

(B)

(C)

(D)

442. Rank the following resonance structures in order of importance from lowest contributor to highest contributor.

$$\ddot{N}{=}C{=}\ddot{O} \qquad \overset{-}{\ddot{N}}{=}\overset{+}{C}{=}\ddot{O} \qquad \ddot{N}{=}\overset{+}{C}{=}\ddot{O}\text{:}^{-}$$

I II III

(A) II < III < I
(B) I < III < II
(C) II < I < III
(D) III < II < I

443. A researcher isolates the product of a reaction and determines it to have a melting point of 112°C. Later, she learned that there was a very small amount of an impurity present with a melting point of 145°C. How does the 112°C melting point compare to the melting point of the pure compound?

(A) It is lower.
(B) It is higher.
(C) It is the same.
(D) It is impossible to determine without knowing the identity of the impurity.

444. Which of the following describes a two-step reaction where the first step is rate determining and the overall process is exothermic?

(A)
E | Reaction coordinate

(B)
E | Reaction coordinate

(C)
E | Reaction coordinate

(D)
E | Reaction coordinate

445. Compound II is in equilibrium with compounds I and III. The following energy profile illustrates this relationship.

Which of the following statements is true?

(A) I forms more rapidly than III; however, III is more stable.
(B) I forms more rapidly than III, and I is more stable.
(C) III forms more rapidly than I; however, I is more stable.
(D) III forms more rapidly than I, and I is more stable.

446. Which of the following is the best representation of the first step in the substitution reaction of 2-bromobutane with cyanide ion?

447. What is the hybridization and bond angles of the indicated atom?

(A) sp^2 and 120°
(B) sp^3 and 109.5°
(C) sp^2 and 90°
(D) sp^3 and 120°

448. Which of the following compounds has the highest boiling point?

(A)

(B)

OH

(C)

NH$_2$

(D)

OH

O

449. Which of the following is the most soluble in cyclohexane?

(A)

COOH

(B)   OH

(C)

(D)

O

450. Which of the following is the strongest acid?

(A) $CH_3CH_2CH_2CH_2OH$
(B) $CH_3CH_2NHCH_2CH_3$
(C) $CH_3CH_2CH_2CH_2NH_2$
(D) $CH_3CH_2CH_2CH_2CH_3$

451. Which of the following compounds yields only one monochloro product upon free radical chlorination?

(A)

(B)

(C)

(D)

452. An organic chemist performs a free radical bromination of 3-methylpentane. Which of the following is the major product?

(A)

Br

(B)

Br

(C)

Br

(D)

Br

453. Many biologically important compounds such as proteins are amides, while others, such as fats, are esters. In the laboratory, the most efficient methods of producing amides and esters use acid chlorides or anhydrides. However, cells use alternate methods. Why is this the case?

(A) Acid chlorides and anhydrides are too reactive to occur in cells.
(B) Acid chlorides and anhydrides cannot cross the lipid bilayer and enter the cell.
(C) Acid chlorides and anhydrides give different products under physiological conditions.
(D) Acid chlorides and anhydrides do not form under physiological conditions.

454. What is the hybridization of atoms I and II in the following compound?

(A) I is sp^3, and II is sp^2.
(B) I is sp^2, and II is sp^2.
(C) I is sp^2, and II is sp^3.
(D) I is sp^3, and II is sp^3.

455. Aromatic compounds react with sodium dissolved in liquid ammonia to give two possible products through the Birch reduction. The reaction and possible products are as follows.

Product I forms if R is electron-donating, and product II forms if R is electron-withdrawing. Why is there a preference for product I or II?

(A) resonance stabilization
(B) induced electrophilic substitution
(C) induced nucleophilic substitution
(D) ease of oxidation

456. The synthesis of many addition polymers begins with an initiator such as benzoyl peroxide. This is the structure of benzoyl peroxide.

The reaction begins with the homolytic cleavage of the O–O bond to form two benzoyl radicals. The benzoyl radical can attack a substituted alkene such as styrene to begin a chain reaction. The attack of the alkene by the benzoyl radical is

(A) a propagation step
(B) an initiation step
(C) a termination step
(D) a complexation step

457. The Kolbe electrolytic synthesis produces hydrocarbons from carboxylic acids. The general reaction is

$$2\ RCOO^- \xrightarrow{\text{electrolysis}} R\text{–}R + 2CO_2$$

What type of reaction is this?

(A) a reduction
(B) an oxidation
(C) a neutralization
(D) a free radical addition

458. The Wacker oxidation can convert terminal alkenes to methyl ketones by the reaction of molecular oxygen. The catalyst is a mixture of palladium and copper chloride. The reaction is

$$\text{R} \diagup\!\!\diagdown\!\!\diagup \quad \xrightarrow[\text{PdCl}_2/\text{CuCl}_2]{\text{O}_2} \quad \underset{\text{R}\qquad\text{CH}_3}{\overset{\text{O}}{\diagup\!\!\diagdown}}$$

What change in the IR spectrum could be used to monitor the progress of the reaction?

(A) the disappearance of a band near 1650 cm^{-1} and the increase in a band near 1715 cm^{-1}

(B) the disappearance of a band near 1650 cm^{-1} and the increase in a band near 3620 cm^{-1}

(C) the disappearance of a band near 2240 cm^{-1} and the increase in a band near 1715 cm^{-1}

(D) the disappearance of a band near 2180 cm^{-1} and the increase in a band near 1715 cm^{-1}

459. Which of the following amino acids CANNOT form a coordinate covalent bond to a metal ion in a metalloenzyme?

(A)

$$H_2N—CH—C(=O)—OH$$
with side chain $CH_2—SH$

(B)

$$H_2N—CH—C(=O)—OH$$
with side chain $(CH_2)_4—NH_2$

(C)

$$H_2N—CH—C(=O)—OH$$
with side chain $CH_2—C(=O)—OH$

(D)

$$H_2N—CH—C(=O)—OH$$
with side chain $CH—CH_3$, CH_3

460. Urea, a metabolic waste product, exists in the following resonance forms.

$$H_2\ddot{N}—C(=\overset{..}{O}:)—\ddot{N}H_2 \longleftrightarrow H_2N=C(—\overset{..}{\overset{..}{O}}:)—\overset{..}{N}H_2 \longleftrightarrow H_2\ddot{N}—C(—\overset{..}{\overset{..}{O}}:)=NH_2$$

Considering all the resonance forms, what are the charges on the oxygen atom and the nitrogen atoms?

(A) O is δ–, and both N's are δ+.
(B) O is δ+, and both N's are δ–.
(C) O is δ–, and both N's are 0.
(D) All atoms have 0 charge.

461. Urea, a metabolic waste product, exists in the following resonance forms.

What is the shape of a urea molecule?

(A) trigonal planar
(B) tetrahedral
(C) trigonal pyramidal
(D) T-shaped

462. The first step in the preparation of TNT (trinitrotoluene) is the mono-nitration of toluene. (The toluene undergoes two additional nitrations to yield the final product.) The first step in the formation of TNT is

What species actually attacks the aromatic ring in this step?

(A) NO_2^+
(B) NO_3^-
(C) H^+
(D) HSO_4^-

463. The first step in the preparation of TNT (trinitrotoluene) is the mono-nitration of toluene. (The toluene undergoes two additional nitrations to yield the final product.) The first step in the formation of TNT is

What is the most likely position for the NO_2 relative to the CH_3?

(A) ortho or para
(B) ortho or meta
(C) meta or para
(D) meta only

464. The melting points for the nitrobenzoic acids are in the following table.

Ortho-nitrobenzoic acid   147°C
Meta-nitrobenzoic acid   140°C
Para-nitrobenzoic acid   242°C

Why is the melting point of para-nitrobenzoic acid so much higher than either of the other two compounds in the table?

(A) Para-nitrobenzoic acid has intermolecular hydrogen bonding, and the other two have intramolecular hydrogen bonding.
(B) Para-nitrobenzoic acid has intramolecular hydrogen bonding, and the other two have intermolecular hydrogen bonding.
(C) Only para-nitrobenzoic acid can participate in hydrogen bonding.
(D) Para-nitrobenzoic acid undergoes an acid-base reaction with the neighboring molecules to form a covalent bond between the molecules.

465. The mononitration of phenol yields a mixture of ortho-nitrophenol and para-nitrophenol. Ideally, what will be the melting point of a mixture containing equal amounts of these two isomers?

(A) below the melting point of the lower melting compound
(B) above the melting point of the higher melting compound
(C) the average of the two melting points
(D) slightly above the average of the two melting points

466. The nitration of benzene is an electrophilic substitution reaction where a nitro group replaces a hydrogen atom. During this reaction, what are the initial, intermediate, and final hybridizations of the carbon atom that is attacked by the nitro group?

(A) sp^2, sp^3, sp^2
(B) sp^2, sp^2, sp^2
(C) sp^2, sp^2, sp^3
(D) sp^3, sp^2, sp^2

467. The presence of a free radical is necessary for a free radical mechanism. Which of the following is a free radical?

(A) NO
(B) OH^-
(C) Cl^-
(D) Cl_2

468. The bond angles in the methyl radical are all 120°. What type of orbital contains the unpaired electron?

(A) p
(B) sp^2
(C) sp^3
(D) s

469. Every amino acid has at least two pK_a values, one for the carboxylic acid group and one for the amino group. Some amino acids have an additional pK_a value for the side chain. For aspartic acid, the pK_a values are 2.1 and 9.8 (carboxylic acid and amino groups, respectively). The side chain has a pK_a of 3.9. What is the predominant structure for aspartic acid at pH 7?

(A)
$$H_2N-CH-C(=O)-OH$$
with side chain $CH_2-C(=O)-OH$

(B)
$$\overset{\oplus}{H_3N}-CH-C(=O)-OH$$
with side chain $CH_2-C(=O)-\overset{\ominus}{O}$

(C)
$$\overset{\oplus}{H_3N}-CH-C(=O)-\overset{\ominus}{O}$$
with side chain $CH_2-C(=O)-\overset{\ominus}{O}$

(D)
$$\overset{\oplus}{H_3N}-CH-C(=O)-\overset{\ominus}{O}$$
with side chain $CH_2-C(=O)-OH$

470. Amino acids contain an amine group and a carboxylic acid group. For this reason, amino acids are classified as amphoteric substances. This classification of amino acids is because

(A) they may behave as either a Lewis acid or an Arrhenius acid
(B) they exist as enantiomeric pairs
(C) they exist as pairs of diastereomers
(D) they may behave as either acids or bases

471. In the vapor phase, chloroacetic acid exists as dimers. A dimer is a pair of strongly interacting molecules. Which of the following is the most likely structure of this dimer?

(A)
$$H_2C-C \begin{matrix} OH \\ O \end{matrix} \quad \begin{matrix} Cl \\ H_2C-C \end{matrix} \begin{matrix} O \\ OH \end{matrix}$$

with Cl on H_2C

(B)
$$H_2C-C \begin{matrix} OH \\ O \end{matrix} \quad \begin{matrix} O \\ HO \end{matrix} C-CH_2 \begin{matrix} Cl \end{matrix}$$

with Cl on H_2C

(C)
$$H_2C-C \begin{matrix} OH \\ O \end{matrix} \quad \begin{matrix} HO \\ O \end{matrix} C-CH_2 \begin{matrix} Cl \end{matrix}$$

with Cl on H_2C

(D)
$$\begin{matrix} O \\ HO \end{matrix} C-CH_2 \begin{matrix} Cl \end{matrix} \quad \begin{matrix} Cl \\ H_2C-C \end{matrix} \begin{matrix} O \\ OH \end{matrix}$$

472. Every amino acid has at least two pK$_a$ values, one for the carboxylic acid group and one for the amino group. Some amino acids have an additional pK$_a$ value for the side chain. Which of the following will have the lowest pK$_a$ for its carboxylic acid group?

(A)
$$H_2N—CH—C(=O)—OH$$
$$|$$
$$CH_2$$
$$|$$
$$CH_2$$
$$|$$
$$C=O$$
$$|$$
$$OH$$

(B)
$$H_2N—CH—C(=O)—OH$$
$$|$$
$$CH_2$$
$$|$$
$$CH—CH_3$$
$$|$$
$$CH_3$$

(C)
$$H_2N—CH—C(=O)—OH$$
$$|$$
$$CH—CH_3$$
$$|$$
$$CH_3$$

(D)
$$H_2N—CH—C(=O)—OH$$
$$|$$
$$CH_3$$

473. As you saw earlier, the following carbohydrate sequence shows the terminal sequence of the Type A determinant protein in blood.

Which of the subunits can change its stereochemistry by mutarotation?

(A) unit A
(B) unit B
(C) unit D
(D) none

474. Condensation polymers form when monomers join through condensation reactions. In a condensation reaction, two groups join with the expulsion of a small molecule such as water. Polymers such as polyesters, nylons, and proteins are examples of condensation polymers. Which of the following is LEAST likely to serve as a monomer for the formation of a condensation polymer?

(A) $CH_3CH_2CH_2OH$
(B) $HOCH_2CH_2COCl$
(C) $H_2NCH_2CH_2C(O)OC(O)CH_2CH_2NH_2$
(D) $HOCH_2CH_2CH_2COOH$

475. Which is the more stable conformer of 1-t-butyl-4-propyl cyclohexane?

(A) Both are equatorial.
(B) The t-butyl is equatorial, and the propyl is axial.
(C) The t-butyl is axial, and the propyl is equatorial.
(D) Both are axial.

476. Which amino acid side chain may undergo hydrolysis during hydrolysis of a protein?

(A) valine
(B) phenylalanine
(C) leucine
(D) asparagine

477. Nylon-66 is a polymer formed from 1,6-diaminohexane and adipic acid (1,6-hexandioic acid). The polymer formed is a

(A) polyamide
(B) polyester
(C) polycarboxylate
(D) polysaccharide

478. The free radical monobromination of (R)-3-ethyl-2,2-dimethylhexane produces

(A) the (S) product
(B) the (R) product
(C) a racemic mixture
(D) the meso product

479. What is the maximum number of products isolated from the following reaction?

(A) 2
(B) 5
(C) 7
(D) 3

480. How many chiral centers are in the following compound?

(A) 5
(B) 7
(C) 3
(D) 4

481. How many σ and π bonds are in the following compound?

(A) 27 σ and 2 π
(B) 19 σ and 2 π
(C) 17 σ and 3 π
(D) 20 σ and 3 π

482. What is the degree of unsaturation in the following molecule?

$$H_2N-CH-C(=O)-OH$$

(with CH_2 substituent connected to an imidazole ring containing N and NH)

(A) 6
(B) 5
(C) 4
(D) 3

483. How many chiral centers are in the following molecule?

C_2H_5, Cl, OH, CH_3, H, H, CH_2-CH_2

(A) 0
(B) 2
(C) 4
(D) 5

484. Which is the correct order of increasing acidity?

(A) sp-hybridized CH bonds < alcohols < phenols < carboxylic acids < sulfonic acids

(B) sp-hybridized CH bonds > alcohols > phenols > carboxylic acids > sulfonic acids

(C) sp-hybridized CH bonds < alcohols ≈ phenols < carboxylic acids ≈ sulfonic acids

(D) sp-hybridized CH bonds ≈ alcohols < phenols ≈ carboxylic acids < sulfonic acids

485. Which of the following is the most stable conformer of butane?

(A)

(B)

(C)

(D)

486. How many monochlorinated isomers (including cis and trans forms) will the following reaction produce?

$$\xrightarrow[\text{hv}]{\text{Cl}_2}$$

(A) 8
(B) 6
(C) 4
(D) 3

487. Which of the following free radicals is the most stable?

(A)

(B)

(C)

(D)

488. It requires a higher temperature to sulfonate benzoic acid than to sulfonate toluene. Why is this true?

(A) The carboxylic acid group is deactivating, and the alkyl group is activating.

(B) The carboxylic acid group is more deactivating than the weakly deactivating alkyl group.

(C) The alkyl group is deactivating, and the carboxylic acid group is activating.

(D) The alkyl group leads to less steric hindrance than the carboxylic acid group.

489. Which of the following is the strongest acid?

(A) HCl

(B) H_2O

(C) HBr

(D) NH_3

490. The complete combustion of 1 mole of octane produces

(A) 8 moles CO_2 and 8 moles H_2O

(B) 16 moles CO_2 and 18 moles H_2O

(C) 8 moles CO_2 and 10 moles H_2O

(D) 8 moles CO_2 and 9 moles H_2O

491. The free radical monochlorination of methylpropane may produce how many different products?

(A) 2
(B) 1
(C) 3
(D) 4

492. One experiment in the investigation of the reaction of ethyl iodide with hydroxide ion found that tripling the concentration of both the ethyl iodide and the hydroxide ion caused the rate to

(A) remain the same
(B) increase × 3
(C) increase × 9
(D) increase × 6

493. The first step in a hydroboration reaction is an attack on an alkene by BH_3. In this case, BH_3 is behaving as

(A) a Lewis acid
(B) a Lewis base
(C) a nucleophile
(D) an Arrhenius acid

494. Which of the following molecules would NOT be a monomer in a polymerization reaction?

(A) $H_2NCH_2CH_2CH_2NH_2$
(B) $HOCH_2CH_2CH_2OH$
(C) $CH_3CH_2CH_2OH$
(D) $HOOC(CH_2)_4COOH$

495. Which of the following is the strongest base?

(A) CH_3^-
(B) OH^-
(C) NH_2^-
(D) OCH_3^-

496. For which of the following molecules is hydrogen bonding an important factor influencing the physical properties?

(A) HBr
(B) CH_2F_2
(C) CH_3CH_3
(D) $NH(CH_3)_2$

497. What is the relationship between the following two molecules?

(A) They are enantiomers.
(B) They are the same.
(C) They are diastereomers.
(D) They are meso.

498. Why is trifluoroacetic acid a stronger acid than trichloroacetic acid?

(A) Fluorine is more electronegative than chlorine; therefore, there is a greater inductive effect.
(B) Chlorine is more electronegative than fluorine; therefore, there is a greater inductive effect.
(C) Fluorine can participate in hydrogen bonding, and chlorine cannot.
(D) Hydrolysis forms hydrofluoric acid, which is a stronger acid than hydrochloric acid.

499. The following equilibria apply to all amino acids.

The central form is the zwitterion form. Which of the following statements is true?

(A) The zwitterion is in equilibrium with the other forms, so it is neither an acid nor a base.
(B) The zwitterion can act either as an acid or as a base.
(C) All three forms can act as a base.
(D) All three forms can act as an acid.

500. It is possible to produce mostly one alkyl halide via the following reaction.

$$\xrightarrow[\text{Peroxides}]{\text{HBr}}$$

Which of the following is the major product of this reaction?

(A) Br

(B) Br

(C) Br

(D) Br

One more. A biochemist plans upon synthesizing a small polypeptide. The synthesis is a three-step process. The experimental percent yields of each of the steps are 90%, 30%, and 70%, respectively. What is the overall percent yield?

(A) 60%
(B) 90%
(C) 30%
(D) 20%

Chapter 1: The Fundamentals

1. (B) Single and double bonds hold all of the carbon atoms in this nanotube together; therefore, the answer is sp^2 hybridization.

2. (A) You can eliminate answers B and D because of the charge separation, and answer A has the lowest formal charges on the atoms. Answer C features 10 electrons around carbon.

3. (D) Structure III is an ionic compound, not a resonance form. Therefore, that eliminates answers A, B, and C.

4. (B) The presence of the highly electronegative fluorine atoms withdraws electron density from the –O-H bond by an induction effect, weakening the bond and therefore increasing the acidity. The more fluorine atoms or the closer the fluorine atoms are to the –OH, the greater the inductive effect and the stronger the acid.

5. (B) The nitrogen atoms are triply bonded to each other. A triple bond involves sp hybridization.

6. (D) In ortho-nitrophenol there is resonance stabilization of the anion formed. There is no comparable stabilization in the case of phenol.

7. (D) Carbon 1 is triply bonded (sp hybridization). Carbon 2 has a single bond to another carbon, two single bonds to hydrogen atoms, and one to a phosphorus atom. Carbon 3 has a double bond to an oxygen and two single bonds, one to another carbon and one to a nitrogen.

8. (A) Answer A is not a cyclohexane but a cyclohexene.

9. (C) The C-C single bonds in 1,3-butadiene are between two sp^2 hybridized carbons (double bonded); therefore, sp^2 hybridized orbitals are utilized.

10. (D) Isomers refer to different compounds having the same molecular formula. Conformers refer to rotation around a single bond. Diastereomers refer to being nonsuperimposable, and not mirror images. Geometric isomers differ in the geometry around a double bond (cis/trans isomers).

11. (B) The triflate anion has the ability to exist in resonance forms with delocalization of the negative charge. This resonance stabilizes the structure, making it more stable than the hydroxide ion and a better leaving group.

12. (B) Here you have a six-carbon backbone with alternating single and double bonds. The bond between C(4) and C(5) is a single bond. Since there are sp^2 bonds on either side of it, this bond has more s-character than the sp^3 hybrid bond in a normal alkane, and therefore it is shorter.

13. (A) The carbon atom is sp^2 hybridized, so it has used one s- and two of the p-orbitals for hybridization and forming three equivalent orbitals. That leaves one unhybridized p-orbital.

14. (A) The acid is a catalyst in the hydrolysis of an ester because changing its concentration has no effect on the reaction, and it is not consumed in the reaction.

15. (D) Bonds 1 and 2 should be of equal lengths since resonance will occur and they will be somewhere between a single and double bond in length. The resonance makes bonds 1 and 2 equal in length. Bond 3 is a double bond (without significant resonance) and will be shorter than bonds 1 and 2.

16. (A) The hydrogen labeled 3 will have the weakest bond (making it most acidic) because of the two carbonyl oxygen withdrawing electron density. In addition, the loss of an H^+ from position 3 leaves a resonance stabilized carbanion. The presence of the two adjacent carbonyls is responsible for the resonance stabilization. The H at position 1 is more acidic than the H at position 2 than the H at position 4 because of the high electronegativity of the fluorine. The adjacent carbonyl, because of resonance, makes hydrogen at position 2 more acidic than the hydrogen at position 1.

17. (B) The carbon-nitrogen triple bond contains 2 π bonds (and 1 σ), each of the double bonds in the ring systems contains a double bond for a total of 6 π bonds, the carbonyl carbon has 1 π bond, and the phosphorus-oxygen double bond contains 1 π bond. That gives a total of 10 π bonds.

18. (C) Amines have a nitrogen atom attached to hydrogen atoms or R-groups. There are two nitrogen atoms present: one a nitrogen-carbon triple bond (nitrile) and the other nitrogen attached to two hydrogen atoms and a carbonyl (amide). There is also a phosphate present.

19. (A) In this compound the alcohol is the more important functional group; therefore, numbering should give it the lowest number (and final position in the name) versus the alkyne. There are six carbons present with a triple bond, and numbering from right to left (centering on the more important alcohol), the alcohol group is at carbon 3, making it a hexyn-3-ol. Since the triple bond is between carbons 5 and 6, it would be a 5-hexyn-3-ol. There are no cis/trans options.

20. **(D)** The ketone is the most important functional group present; therefore, numbering should give it the lowest number (and final position in the name) versus the alcohol or alkene. The presence of the ketone group leads to a *-one* suffix. The chain is seven carbons in length with the ketone at carbon 3 and the double bond between positions 4 and 5, so it would be a 4-hepten-3-one. There is a methyl at position 2 and a hydroxyl at the position 6, making it a 6-hydroxy-2-methyl-4-hepten-3-one. Immediately reject answer C since the suffix *-al* is for an aldehyde, not a ketone.

21. **(B)** Benzene has six carbon-to-carbon σ bonds and six carbon-to-hydrogen σ (single bonds). In addition, there are three π bonds in the ring system (one per double bond). Resonance does not alter the total.

22. **(A)** To be saturated, there would need to be 22 hydrogen atoms, not 14. The degree of unsaturation would be $(22 - 14)/2 = 4$, so there would be a total of four π bonds and rings. Hydrogenation attacks π bonds; therefore, there are two π bonds. With the possible answers, the only reasonable one is two π bonds leaving two rings.

23. **(C)** An alcohol, an ether, and an alkene (with an oxygen-containing functional group) can exist, but an acid anhydride requires three oxygen atoms in the structure. An alkene could also contain an ether, alcohol, or carbonyl group.

24. **(D)** The C-N bond length will be related to the bond order (single, double, and triple). In CN^-, there is a triple bond, a very short bond; in OCN^- you have a C=N, a longer bond (slightly changed by resonance), and in the methylamine you have a single bond, the longest.

25. **(B)** The cis term refers to orientation about a carbon-to-carbon double bond. Of the remaining answers, the most stable conformation is the one that maximizes the distance between the groups—the anti conformation.

26. **(B)** The compound is a heptene (seven-carbon backbone, with a double bond). Numbering to give the double bond the lowest possible number makes it a 3-heptene and having the R-groups on the same side of the double bond makes it a (Z).

27. **(D)** The longest chain has seven carbon atoms and only single bonds, which makes it a heptane. There are three methyl groups attached to the heptane, making it a trimethylheptane. Numbering from the end that gives the methyl groups the lowest numbers gives the answer.

28. **(A)** The longest chain has six carbon atoms and only single bonds, which makes it a hexane. The two substituents (bromo and chloro) alphabetically give bromochlorohexane. Numbering from the end that gives the substituents the lowest numbers gives the answer.

29. **(C)** An acid anhydride consists of two carbonyl groups linked by an oxygen atom.

30. (C) The isomers are n-hexane, 2-methylpentane, 3-methylpentane, 2,2-dimethylbutane, and 2,3-dimethylbutane.

31. (D) An isobutyl group is a 2-methylpropyl.

32. (A) The nitrogen adjacent to a carbonyl is an amide. Two carbon atoms make this a substituted acetamide. The –OH group is para (#4) on the phenyl ring. The ring is attached to the N, making it an N-.

33. (B) The chain splits at the oxygen. There are five carbon atoms to the left (*pent*) and three carbon atoms to the right (*prop*). An oxygen atom adjacent to a carbonyl can be an ester (-*oate* suffix). The acid side of the ester has the carbonyl group. The part of an ester derived from a five-carbon chain is a pentanoate with the carbonyl carbon being 1. If the carbonyl carbon is 1, then the fluorine is on 4. Combining these gives a 4-fluoropentanoate. The propyl group, from the alcohol, remains and according to the nomenclature rules, is the first part of the name.

34. (D) Every ring is one degree of unsaturation, and every π bond is one degree of unsaturation. Answer A gives 3, answer B gives 3, answer C gives 3, and answer D gives 4.

35. (A) This is the only reduction (the only answer where the oxidation state is reduced).

36. (D) The longest chain has seven carbon atoms and only single bonds; therefore, this is a heptane. The branches are methyl, bromo, and hydroxyl (alcohol). The alcohol has highest priority; therefore, this is an alcohol with the –OH being closest to the end of the chain. This gives heptan-2-ol. Following through on the numbering will yield 4-bromo and 5-methyl. Adding these to the root name (alphabetically) gives the answer.

37. (D) An acetal is $R_2C(OR)_2$. The R's may be the same or different.

38. (C) The compound has an eight-carbon backbone with a double bond (octene) and a carboxylic acid group (octenoic acid). Numbering starts at the end closest to the acid end (2-octenoic acid), and the R-groups are oriented on opposite sides of the double bond, making it an (E) conformation.

39. (A) Starting with an isopropylhexane basic structure and then placing the double bond in different positions gives you five different positions on the backbone, with three of those having cis/trans isomers associated (5 + 3) and then two positions for the double bond on the isopropyl group (5 + 3 + 2 = 10).

40. (D) If the compound were saturated, it would have 2(14) + 2 = 30 hydrogen atoms, instead of 14. The degree of unsaturation is (30 – 14)/2 = 8.

41. (A) The compound can be a bromocyclopropane or a 1-bromopropene (cis or trans). But it cannot be a cis- or trans-2-bromopropene, because it will be attached to the carbon with the methyl group and there are only hydrogen atoms on the other carbon—therefore, no cis- or trans- isomers are possible.

42. (B) In general, the "largest" substituent on a cyclohexane ring should be equatorial because there is less steric hindrance in this position.

43. (C) These are structural isomers of each other.

44. (D) There are five on the ring containing the nitrogen, one on the methyl attached to the nitrogen, and two in the ethyl group, for a total of eight.

45. (C) Answer D is a four-membered ring (90° bond angle) and would have more bond strain than the other compounds, which are cyclohexanes. Answers A and B are the chair forms with a great deal of steric interaction because the groups are close. This is not the case in answer C, which is in the chair form.

46. (A) All of the nitrogen atoms indicated have a lone pair of electrons on the nitrogen. Nitrogen I is triple bonded and has a lone pair, indicating sp hybridization; nitrogen II has three single bonds and a lone pair, indicating sp^3 hybridization; and nitrogen III has a double bond, a single bond, and a lone pair, indicating sp^2 hybridization.

47. (A) HCl is a strong acid and will be stronger than any of the organic acids. II will be the next strongest due to considerable resonance stabilization of the anion (conjugate base). I is next, due to minor resonance stabilization of the anion. III is an alcohol with no resonance stabilization possible, so it is the weakest acid.

48. (C) Carbon 1 has three groups around it, giving a trigonal planar geometry (120°).

49. (A) The methyl cation has three groups around it, corresponding to sp^2 hybridization, leaving an unhybridized p-orbital to interact. The methyl anion would have four groups, three bonding pairs, and one nonbonding pair, corresponding to sp^3 hybridization.

50. (C) The two compounds are not mirror images of each other, so they cannot be enantiomers. They are not nonmirror image stereoisomers, so they are not diastereomers. They are not conformers, because that refers to the free rotation around a double bond. They are regioisomers, or positional isomers, differing in the position of the groups attached to the double-bonded carbon.

51. (B) In conjugated systems like this one, the C-C single bonds are commonly shorter than normal ones, because of the partial overlap of the unhybridized p-orbitals of the two adjacent carbons, which leads to resonance.

52. (C) The trans isomer would be the most stable (lower energy). The cis isomer is the least stable (steric hindrance with the groups attached to the double-bonded carbons), and therefore, it is the higher energy form and will release more energy upon hydrogenation.

53. (A) The degree of unsaturation is unaffected by oxygen. For the compound to be unsaturated there would have to be $2 \times 6 + 2 = 14$ hydrogen atoms, instead of 10. The degree of unsaturation would be $(14 - 10)/2 = 2$.

Chapter 2: Isomers and Physical Properties

54. (A) The presence of the lone pair on the nitrogen atom leads to the formation of the double bond to it (N = X), and the nitrogen is best able to accommodate the positive charge.

55. (D) Assign the priorities to each atom (Br > F > -CH_2-C- > CH_3). Then see if the Br →F → etc. rotation is to the right (R) or to the left (S). Answer D has the proper absolute configuration on each atom.

56. (B) These are enantiomers.

57. (D) The trans fluorine atoms cancel, while in all other cases the fluorine atoms do not cancel.

58. (A) Enantiomers only differ in the way they affect plane-polarized light and in their interactions with other optically active substances.

59. (A) To determine the absolute configuration about a carbon atom, note the lowest priority group and assign priority to the other groups. Beginning with the highest priority group, count toward the next highest group and end with the lowest group. Counting to the right (clockwise) is R, and counting to the left (counterclockwise) is S. The configuration about each carbon atom is independent of the configuration around the other carbon atom. The carbon with the two carbons attached is not a stereocenter. For one carbon, you would count to the left (S), and for the other you count to the right (R).

60. (D) The nitrogen can undergo inversion; therefore, it is rapidly changing from one orientation to the opposite orientation.

61. (C) Each racemic mixture would contain two enantiomers: A, B and C, D. The possible combinations of products would then be AC, AD, BC, and BD, for a total of four products.

62. (D) Diastereomers can be easily separated from each other, whereas none of the others can be easily separated, if at all.

63. (C) To determine the absolute configuration about a carbon atom, note the lowest priority group and assign priority to the other groups. Beginning with the highest priority group (Cl in this case), count toward the next highest group and end with the lowest group. Counting to the right (clockwise) is R, and counting to the left (counterclockwise) is S. The configuration about each carbon atom is independent of the configuration around the other carbon atom. Doing this, both carbons turn out to be S.

64. (C) Compound I is nonpolar because all four groups are the same. That eliminates answers A and D. Both II and III are polar and have nonzero dipole moments.

65. (A) Carbonyls are very polar, ethers are slightly polar, and alcohols are somewhere in between those two.

66. (A) Answer B is a hydrocarbon, so it will not be very soluble in water at all. Answer D can form very weak dipole attractions, but these are not strong enough to ensure good solubility. Both answers A and C can undergo hydrogen bonding with water, but the alcohol will form stronger hydrogen bonds because oxygen's electronegativity is greater than nitrogen's. Therefore, the alcohol will be the most soluble.

67. (D) Compounds I and II have the highly electronegative oxygen atom in their structure that allows them to hydrogen bond to water. Remember, hydrogen bonding involves a nitrogen atom, oxygen atom, or a fluorine atom.

68. (C) To determine the absolute configuration about a carbon atom, note the lowest priority group and assign priority to the other groups. Beginning with the highest priority group, count toward the next highest group and end with the lowest group. Counting to the right (clockwise) is R, and counting to the left (counterclockwise) is S. The configuration about each carbon atom is independent of the configuration around the other carbon atom. In answers A, B, and D the stereocenters are R, but it is S in answer C.

69. (D) In answer D, all stereocenters have been inverted, allowing it to be a nonsuperimposable mirror image of the compound. That is not true of the others, because not all of the stereocenters have been inverted.

70. (A) Meso compounds are ones that contain two or more stereocenters. The compound is superimposable with its mirror image. A symmetry plane splits a meso compound. Compounds B, C, and D are superimposable, but compound A cannot be.

71. (A) Achiral compounds are those that are superimposable on their mirror images. I and II cannot be superimposed, but III can. It is a meso compound, as the chlorine atoms are cis, creating a symmetry plane between them.

72. (D) To determine the absolute configuration about a carbon atom, note the lowest priority group and assign priority to the other groups. Beginning with the highest priority group, count toward the next highest group and end with the lowest group. Counting to the right (clockwise) is R, and counting to the left (counterclockwise) is S. The configuration about each carbon atom is independent of the configuration around the other carbon atom. Doing this shows that compound IV has an R stereocenter.

73. (B) Compounds A, C, and D are symmetrical compounds and cannot be polar. In compound B, the hydrocarbon groups around the double bonds are on the same side of the double bond (Z form), and this allows the compound to be very slightly polar.

74. (B) Sodium sulfate is a soluble ionic compound, so its solubility will be greater than the other compounds even though they can all hydrogen bond to water.

75. (D) The boiling point of a compound is highly influenced by the intermolecular forces between the compounds. The stronger the intermolecular forces, the higher the boiling point. Compound I can hydrogen bond to other molecules, while compound II can use only weaker dipole-dipole forces.

76. **(A)** These two structures are diastereomers of each other, not mirror images. The left one is S and S around its stereocenters, while the right is S and R.

77. **(C)** These two compounds are mirror images of each other, making them enantiomers.

78. **(A)** N1 has only single bonds (three of them); therefore, it is sp^3 hybridization. N2 has a double bond and a single bond, which indicates sp^2 hybridization. Each nitrogen atom has a lone pair (not shown).

79. **(A)** There are three chiral carbon atoms ($n = 3$) on the ring containing the oxygen, so there are $2^n = 8$ stereoisomers.

80. **(D)** You are told that both have a chiral center; there is no way to determine the relationship (+ or −) of either compound. Changing atoms (F for Cl) may or may not retain the + or −. There is no information given or predictable about the type (direction) of the rotation.

81. **(C)** It is necessary to determine the absolute configuration about a carbon atom by noting the lowest priority group (in both of these cases an H) and assign priority to the other groups. In this case, the highest priority group on each C is the OH group, followed by the COOH group. Beginning with the highest priority group (OH here), count toward the next highest group (COOH here) and end with the lowest group. Counting to the right (clockwise) is R, and counting to the left (counterclockwise) is S. The configuration about each carbon atom is independent of the configuration around the other carbon atom. Doing this indicates that both carbons are R.

82. **(B)** There are two stereocenters ($n = 2$) on isoleucine, carbons 2 and 3, giving $2^n = 4$ stereoisomers.

83. **(A)** The optical rotation might be changed or not be changed; therefore, it is impossible to determine the effect without more information.

84. **(A)** It is necessary to determine the absolute configuration about a carbon atom by noting the lowest priority group (in the first and third carbons it is an H, and in the second case it is an ethyl group) and assigning priority to the other groups. In this case, the highest priority group on each C is the R group containing the ether group followed by the OCH_3 group. Beginning with the highest priority group, count toward the next highest group (OCH_3 here) and end with the lowest group. Counting to the right (clockwise) is R, and counting to the left (counterclockwise) is S. The configuration about each carbon atom is independent of the configuration around the other carbon atom. Doing this indicates that both carbons 1 and 2 (counting from right to left) are R and the third is S.

85. **(D)** The molecules are the same. Rotating the right-hand structure until the $-OCH_3$ is vertical yields the same structure as the left-hand structure.

86. **(C)** Meso refers to a plane of symmetry in an enantiomer; that is not the question that was posed. The term *archival* refers to having superimposable mirror images, again not the question here. Absolute configuration uses the R and S notation. To determine the absolute configuration about a carbon atom, note the lowest priority group (in this case it is a hydrogen atom) and assign priority to the other groups. In this case, the highest priority group on each C is the R group containing the carbonyl group, next is the group containing the nitrogen, and then the hydrocarbon group. Beginning with the highest priority group, count toward the next highest group and end with the lowest group. Counting to the right (clockwise) is R, and counting to the left (counterclockwise) is S. The configuration about each carbon atom is independent of the configuration around the other carbon atom. Doing this, the direction of rotation is to the left (counterclockwise) and so it is S.

87. (A) These two molecules are identical. Rotating the right-hand structure allows you to place it over the left-hand structure.

88. (D) There is no chiral center in this compound (eliminating answer C), and trans isomers are not more reactive (eliminating answer A). Stability in this case is related to proximity of the groups to each other (steric hindrance). The most stable isomer will be the one in which the groups are as far away from each other as possible—the trans form.

89. (A) In order to convert from one isomer to another, the double bond (π bond) would have to be broken. This is not easy to do and still maintain the structure of the molecule.

90. (C) 1,3,5-hexatriene contains three double bonds (triene). It takes one mole of hydrogen per mole of double bonds. Two moles of the triene will contain six moles of double bonds and will require six moles of hydrogen gas.

91. (D) A mixture of equal amounts of the D and L enantiomers is called a racemic mixture. It would not be optically active (eliminating answer A); *mesomeric* and *diastereometric* are not terms used to describe enantiomers.

92. (C) Meso compounds have stereocenters but also have symmetry that allow them to be the mirror images of themselves. This may occur when you have at least two stereocenters.

93. (A) R and S refer to configurations, not rotations of plane-polarized light. If the light is being rotated to the left (counterclockwise), it is levorotatory; and if it rotates the light to the right (clockwise), it is dextrorotatory.

94. (C) If you have the same number of moles of each enantiomer with equal but opposite rotation, then the result will be no net rotation or 0°. This is a racemic mixture.

95. (B) A chiral center has four different groups attached to it. In 2,3-dibromopentane, there are two chiral centers, the carbon atoms with bromine atoms. Each of those carbons has two different R-groups, a hydrogen atom and a bromine atom attached to it.

96. (A) Enantiomers have the same physical properties, except for their ability to rotate plane-polarized light. Therefore, their melting points will be the same.

97. (A) It is impossible to know what the optical rotation of the product will be. The mechanism does cause inversion of the configuration; however, this does not mean inversion of optical rotation.

98. (A) The difference between a carboxylic acid and its sodium salt would be the reaction with a base to form the carboxylate ion. This does not affect the chiral center and cannot affect the rotation.

99. (D) There are four chiral centers ($n = 4$) in this molecule. The number of possible isomers is 2^n, or 2^4 in this case, $2^4 = 16$.

100. (A) The number of meso forms does not affect the number of stereoisomers, just the number of chiral centers. The number of isomers may be calculated by the formula 2^n.

101. (B) Diastereomers may have different physical properties, but their molecular formulas must be the same.

102. (D) Enantiomers have opposite configurations and optical rotations. Therefore, compound C would have an S absolute configuration and a negative optical rotation.

103. (D) The two compounds are cis/trans isomers (or diastereomers), and as such, they are expected to have different physical properties altogether. There are differences in one chiral center, so there would be a difference in the optical activity.

104. (C) To determine the absolute configuration about a carbon atom, note the lowest priority group (in both carbons in the ring, it is a hydrogen) and assign priority to the other groups. In the case of both carbons it is the nitrogen group, followed by the isopropyl. Beginning with the highest priority group, count toward the next highest group and end with the lowest group. Counting to the right (clockwise) is R, and counting to the left (counterclockwise) is S. The configuration about each carbon atom is independent of the configuration around the other carbon atom. Doing this the direction of rotation is to the left (counterclockwise), and so it is S for both.

105. (D) In order to have hydrogen bonding, there must be a hydrogen atom attached to an extremely electronegative element: O, N, or F. The only structures that meet that criteria are the alcohol and the amine, III and IV.

106. (A) To determine the absolute configuration about a carbon atom, note the lowest priority group (in both of these cases an H) and assign priority to the other groups. In this case, the highest priority group on each C is the Br group, followed by the ethyl, and then the methyl group. Beginning with the highest priority group (Br here), count toward the next highest group (ethyl here) and end with the lowest group. Counting to the right (clockwise) is R, and counting to the left (counterclockwise) is S. The configuration about each carbon atom is independent of the configuration around the other carbon atom. Doing this indicates that structure I is R and structure II is S.

107. (B) The chlorine atoms are in different positions relative to the aldehyde group; therefore, this makes the two compounds not identical, conformers, or enantiomers.

108. (A) Meso compounds have stereocenters, and there is a plane of symmetry splitting the molecule. In I and IV, there is no plane of symmetry present. In II, there is a plane of symmetry between the two chiral centers. In III, there is a symmetry plane cutting the molecule in two.

109. (D) Compound I can form two hydrogen bonds, II cannot form any hydrogen bonds, and III can form one hydrogen bond. The one with the greatest number of hydrogen bonds will have the greatest boiling point and so on. The carbonyl group adds to the attraction between the molecules, but not enough to compensate for the second hydrogen bond in the diol.

110. (C) The boiling point is related to the strength of the intermolecular forces; the stronger the force, the higher the boiling point. Structure I can undergo strong hydrogen bonding, whereas structure II has weaker dipole-dipole forces.

111. (C) All of the compounds except II have different substituent groups, on the ring system. However, II has the same groups, and this leads to a plane of symmetry (the cyclobutene ring)—the plane of the molecule.

112. (B) Achiral compounds are mirror images that are superimposable. Answer B has an internal plane of symmetry, which allows it to be superimposed on its mirror image. Answer B is a meso compound.

113. (A) The 0° optical rotation indicates an achiral, a meso, or a racemic mixture. If it were an achiral reacting with S stereoisomers, you would get only one compound. A meso compound reacting with S stereoisomers yields a racemic mixture with a single melting point. If it is a racemic mixture reacting with an S stereoisomer, it would yield two diastereomers with different melting points and be easily separated. The cis isomer would probably give only one product.

114. (D) There are eight chiral carbon atoms ($n = 8$) present, so the number of optical isomers would be $2^8 = 256$.

115. (B) The (+) and (–) are optical rotations, not absolute configurations, so answers C and D can be eliminated. To determine the absolute configuration about a carbon atom, note the lowest priority group and assign priority to the other groups. Beginning with the highest priority group, count toward the next highest group and end with the lowest group. Counting to the right (clockwise) is R, and counting to the left (counterclockwise) is S. The configuration about each carbon atom is independent of the configuration around the other carbon atom. In this case, it would be counting counterclockwise (S).

116. (D) Meso compounds are ones that contain two or more stereocenters that are superimposable with its mirror image. Answer C has no stereocenter. Answer D has stereocenters and a plane of symmetry between them, which allows it to be superimposable with its mirror image.

Chapter 3: Substitution and Elimination Reactions

117. (D) There is only one hydrogen atom to be replaced for substitution to yield the 2-chloro-2-methylpropane and nine hydrogen atoms that can be replaced to give the 1-chloro-2-methylpropane. Therefore, (36%/1 H) : (64% / 9 H) ≈ 5 : 1.

118. (A) One Li leaves with the halogen, and the other replaces the halogen on the ring.

119. (B) The alkoxide has a lone pair of electrons. Therefore, it acts as the nucleophile and attacks the carbon atom with the alcohol –OH attached.

120. (C) There are four different, nonequivalent carbons on 2-methylbutane in which monochlorination can take place.

121. (A) The starting structure is a primary alcohol, and the reactants will cause oxidation of this alcohol, yielding a carboxylic acid. The conditions are such that partial oxidation to the aldehyde is not the final product.

122. (B) Oxidation of a secondary alcohol yields a ketone.

123. (A) The initial compound is a tertiary alkyl halide. Tertiary alkyl halides react by an S_N1 mechanism, so that the bromide leaves, with the formation of the carbonium ion shown in answer A. Answers B and C are S_N2 mechanisms, which are not important to tertiary alkyl halides. Answer D is a less stable secondary carbonium ion.

124. (B) Answers C and D would be intermediates associated with an S_N1 reaction, not an S_N2. Answers A and B are S_N2, the nucleophile is negative (or $\delta-$), eliminating answer A.

125. (C) Ammonia would be the best leaving group because it is a stable neutral molecule. The others would have an attraction between the anion and the group left behind.

126. (D) The leaving group in answer D would be N_2. Diatomic nitrogen, N_2, is the most stable, and it is also neutral, unlike the other leaving groups.

127. (A) In the propagation step, you have the formation of free radicals beginning with a free radical. Answer D is an initiation step (creating a free radical from a molecule), and answers B and C are both termination steps (combining two free radicals to yield a molecule).

128. (C) Tertiary free radicals are more stable than secondary, primary, or aromatic ones. In addition, this free radical is also resonance stabilized.

129. (D) The replacement of the tertiary hydrogen would proceed by the formation of a stable tertiary free radical.

130. (B) Structures B and C are primary, which favors an S_N2 mechanism, because there is less steric hindrance, but Br is a much better leaving group than F.

131. (C) Only primary and secondary alcohols undergo oxidation; answers A and D are primary alcohols, and answer B is a secondary alcohol. Answer C is a tertiary alcohol and will not undergo oxidation by acidic $K_2Cr_2O_7$.

132. (A) Secondary and tertiary alcohols react with strong acids via S_N1 reactions. I and III are tertiary alcohols. II and IV are primary alcohols.

133. (B) After dehydration of the 2-methyl-1-pentanol, there is a rearrangement to give a more stable carbocation intermediate, which leads to II.

134. (D) Free radical bromination is VERY selective—it will substitute on the tertiary carbon more than a secondary one, which substitutes more than primary carbon. IV has a tertiary carbon.

135. (B) Structure II is more stable than I due to steric considerations. In structure II the two groups are equatorial, minimizing the repulsion.

136. (A) In order for a substance to be a nucleophile, it should (1) have a center of high electron density. Therefore, a negative charge is a stronger nucleophile than a neutral species or one with a positive charge. (2) the lower on the periodic table, the stronger the nucleophile. Therefore, $HSe^- > HS^-$.

137. (A) The stronger base will have the higher electron density on the oxygen on the carbonyl carbon. The chlorine atoms on the trichloroacetate ion tend to withdraw electron density from the oxygen atoms attached to the carbonyl carbon (inductive effect). This makes the trichloroacetate ion a weaker base than the acetate ion.

138. (A) Carbocation stability is related to the degree of alkyl substitution on the carbon on which the positive charge is located. The higher the degree of substitution, the more stable the ion is. Structure I is a primary carbocation, II is a tertiary, and III is a secondary. The least stable is I, followed by III, and the most stable will be II.

139. (B) Carbocations exhibit sp^2 hybridization and a trigonal planar geometry in order to minimize electron repulsion.

140. (A) Inversion of configuration takes place with S_N2 reactions (eliminating answer B) and there are changes in conformation (eliminating answer C). The intermediate in S_N1 reactions with chiral compounds is an achiral structure, which may be attacked from either side to give a racemic mixture and not an achiral product.

141. (D) S_N2 reactions do have second-order kinetics (two substances involved in the rate-determining step), which is basically a one-step reaction with a five-coordinate intermediate with the structure undergoing substitution. However, there is no carbocation formation—that is, in S_N1 reactions.

142. (B) E1 reactions are unimolecular, so the kinetics are first order. A double bond will form, so there is a π bond, and it is a two-step mechanism: formation of the transition state and then the alkene. There is no attack by another species, certainly not a nucleophile.

143. (C) In the E2 reaction there is deprotonation by a base, loss of the leaving group, rehybridization of the reacting carbon center from sp^3 to sp^2 hybridization, and the formation of a double bond (π bond). There is no carbocation intermediate.

144. (A) Halogenations (chlorination) of an alkane takes place by a free radical mechanism including initiation, propagation, and termination steps.

145. (D) Since the solvent lowers the reaction rate, it probably is interacting with the nucleophile by solvating it, making it more difficult to attack an electrophile. The solvent should cause none of the other changes listed.

146. (C) The reaction mechanism stayed S_N2. Optical activity is not related to the rate of reaction. The stability of the products is a thermodynamic argument and not a kinetic argument. The rate depends on the reactants and activated complex (activation energy). The reason that the rate decreased was that the activation energy for the reaction increased. Watch out for mixed kinetic-thermodynamic problems on the MCAT. In general, it is not possible to use kinetics to explain a thermodynamic question or to use thermodynamics to explain a kinetic question.

147. (A) The reaction of methyl bromide will follow an S_N2 mechanism. First-order kinetics is incorrect—S_N1 is not S_N2. Formation of a racemic mixture is incorrect, because that would require a chiral carbon, something impossible with methyl bromide. S_N2 reactions have an inversion of structure, which means the conformation is not retained. S_N2 reactions, however, exhibit second-order kinetics, because there are two reacting species in the rate-determining step.

148. (B) In a termination step there is a combination of free radicals that stops the reaction. Answers A and C are propagation steps because a free radical forms from a free radical; answer D is an initiation step because a molecule generates free radicals.

149. (D) S_N2 reaction mechanisms are not first-order reactions with respect to the reaction kinetics. S_N2 reactions exhibit second-order kinetics (the reason for the 2 in the name), because there are two reacting species in the rate-determining step.

150. (B) The reaction between ethyl iodide and the hydroxide is an S_N2 reaction; these reactions obey second-order kinetics: first order with the alkyl halide and first order with the hydroxide. Doubling the concentration of the hydroxide will cause the rate to double.

151. (A) In S_N1 reactions, first-order kinetics applies. The rate is first order with respect to the concentration of the substrate because only the substrate is in the rate-determining step.

152. (D) S_N2 reactions obey second-order kinetics, so the concentration of the nucleophile is important. There is inversion, so there is no retention of configuration, and S_N2 reactions are a one-step process, not two. However, primary alkyl halides do react faster than either secondary or tertiary alkyl halides.

153. (A) The free radical chlorination of an alkane gives many products. It is not a very selective reaction (nonregioselective), and factors such as inductive effects and statistical factors will affect the products formed and their proportions. A number of products, not just the most stable, will form.

154. (A) Initiation (generation of the free radical) is the first step in all free radical mechanisms.

155. (A) S_N2 mechanisms are very susceptible to steric interference. Smaller is better. The remaining factors should be the same for the two alkyl halides.

156. (A) This is a tertiary alkyl halide; therefore, the reaction will follow an S_N1 mechanism. An S_N1 mechanism on a chiral center normally yields a racemic mixture.

157. (A) This is an electrophilic attack on a conjugated system, which leads to 1,4-addition. The 3-chloro product is the Markovnikov product. The other product results from resonance of the intermediate allylic cation. (The intermediate allylic cation also leads to some of the 3-chloro product.)

158. (B) In order for a substance to be a nucleophile, it should (1) have a center of high electron density. Therefore, a negative charge is a stronger nucleophile than a neutral species or one with a positive charge. (2) The farther to the left on the periodic table, the stronger the nucleophile. Therefore, $NH_2^- > OH^-$.

159. (D) The reaction condition leads to carbene formation. Answer D is the product of a carbene addition to a double bond.

160. (A) An S_N2 attack on a secondary alkyl halide requires a strong nucleophile to attack the alkyl halide.

161. (A) Larger groups and more branching will lead to steric problems, which is particularly noticeable in an S_N2 mechanism.

162. (C) Answer B is incorrect since the substitution does not occur at the least sterically hindered site. There is no chance of resonance with this structure, and it is not the site with the most $\delta+$. However, inductive effects, leading to monobromination, can stabilize the intermediate. Bromine is VERY selective, and a tertiary alkyl halide is strongly preferred.

163. (B) In free radical addition reactions, the propagation step involves a free radical (i.e., the chlorine free radical) reacting with the substrate (i.e., methane) to produce another free radical (i.e., the methyl free radical). An initiation step generates two free radicals from a molecule, and a termination step generates a molecule from two free radicals. Carbocations are never involved.

164. (C) S_N1 reactions are first order in the substrate concentration. Therefore, doubling the concentration of the sodium ethoxide (the nucleophile) will have no effect on the reaction rate.

165. (A) Neopentyl bromide, along with ethyl, methyl, and propyl bromide, are all 1° bromides and will yield a 1° carbocation (rearrangement may occur). However, isopropyl bromide is a 2° bromide, which will yield a 2° carbocation, which is more stable than a 1° one.

166. (D) Tertiary alkyl halides react exclusively by S_N1 mechanisms, and answer D is the only tertiary alkyl halide present.

167. (B) Free radical stability is related to the degree of alkyl substitution on the carbon on which the single electron resides. The least stable is the methyl group itself, then primary, then secondary, and finally, tertiary is the most stable. Structure III is a tertiary, so it will be the most stable. Structures II and IV are both secondary, so they should be approximately the same, and structure I is a primary, so it will be the least stable.

168. (A) To increase the acid strength of phenol, electron density needs to be withdrawn from the O-H bond. Weakening the bond makes it easier to break, and therefore it is a stronger acid. Both the cyano and the trichloromethyl groups are electron-withdrawing groups due to the high electronegativities of the nitrogen and chlorine atoms. Therefore, they will make the acid stronger.

169. (C) Configuration II, the eclipsed configuration, is the least stable because of steric interactions. Configuration III, gauche, is the most stable due to intramolecular hydrogen bonding. Configuration I, anti, is the second best in terms of stability. If there were no intramolecular hydrogen bonding, configuration I would be the most stable.

170. (A) The free radical chlorination of isopentane will yield all possible products shown because the chlorine radicals can attack any position. The distribution of the products will not be equal.

171. (C) Strong acids react with primary alcohols via S_N2 mechanisms. II and IV are primary alcohols, while I and III are tertiary alcohols. Tertiary alcohols never react via an S_N2 mechanism.

172. (A) This is a dehydrohalogenation with the more stable (more substituted) alkene forming. Structure A is the most substituted. Structure B has a five-bonded carbon atom, which will not form.

173. (A) This is a free radical halogenation, and bromine is very selective and goes to the tertiary carbon.

174. (B) The product of this reaction is formed by an S_N2 reaction with inversion of configuration and no rearrangement—structure II.

175. (B) These conditions will lead to the replacement of the OH with a Br.

176. (B) A nucleophile has a lone pair of electrons; in answers A, C, and D, there is a lone pair on the nitrogen. This is not true in answer B, since all electrons are in bonds.

177. (C) There would be a carbocation intermediate formed in the reaction, and water, because of its polar nature, would stabilize the carbocation better than the less polar DMF solvent.

178. (C) The reaction of a primary alcohol with $SOCl_2$ yields an alkyl halide, answer C.

179. (D) Answer C is a primary alcohol, answers A and B are secondary ones, and answer D is a tertiary. Tertiary alcohols undergo dehydration faster than secondary alcohols, with primary alcohols being the slowest. Since two of the alcohols are secondary, it is unlikely that either will be the answer.

Chapter 4: Electrophilic Addition Reactions

180. (C) These two compounds, p-toluenesulfonic acid and o-toluenesulfonic acid, are constitutional (structural) isomers since they differ in where a group is attached.

181. (A) During this reaction you go from three double bonds to one, loss of two π bonds. Those two double bonds were converted to a single bond, thereby gaining two σ bonds.

182. (D) The intermediate will be a carbonium ion since you are starting with a conjugated diene. This will be a 1,4-electrophilic addition reaction.

183. (B) HI is the strongest acid of those shown. The strongest acid gives the fastest reaction because protonation of the alkene is the rate-determining step.

184. (A) This is an elimination reaction (E2) with a hindered base. There will be no substitution product D or C. Products A and B are both E2 products. The hindered base leads to the preference of product A over product B (Hofmann rule over Zaitsev rule).

185. (D) Structure I has an activating group attached, and III has a deactivating group attached. I should be the fastest, followed by II, and III will be the slowest.

186. (B) The ketone adjacent to the ring is a meta-director, so the product will be answer B. (In addition, o,p-directors tend to produce two products unless there are serious steric problems.)

187. (C) This is an addition reaction that should be a Markovnikov addition, as shown in answer C. Answer A is a free radical product and can be eliminated, answer B is the result of an anti-Markovnikov addition and can be eliminated, and answer D would not be a product of this reaction.

188. (A) This is an anti-addition under these conditions, resulting in a racemic mixture.

189. (D) The mCPBA forms oxacyclopropane rings, starting trans and ending trans. Answer D is trans, and answer B is cis.

190. (A) The OsO_4 promotes vicinal-syn-dihydroxylation of double bonds, resulting in compound A. Answer D is the anti compound.

191. (B) The first step is hydroboration, and the second is oxidation to the alcohol. The reaction combination gives an anti-Markovnikov addition.

192. (C) Ozonolysis cleaves the double bond and gives carbonyl groups. The other product would be formaldehyde.

193. (A) Hydrogenation using a Lindlar catalyst yields a cis alkene.

194. (C) The N-containing group (amide) is para-directing, so compound C (the para isomer) is formed.

195. (D) This is a Friedel-Crafts acylation reaction. The isopropyl group is an o,p-director, but steric hindrance is great at the ortho position, so that the para product predominates over the ortho product.

196. (B) The Hückel rule states that in cyclic systems the compound is aromatic if there are $4n + 2$ π electrons. Answer A has 14 π electrons ($n = 3$) and is aromatic; answer C has 18 π electrons ($n = 4$) and is aromatic; answer D has 4 π electrons ($n = 1$) and is aromatic; answer B has 16 π electrons and does not fit the Hückel rule and therefore is not aromatic.

197. (A) By Hückel's rule, a cyclic conjugated polyene may be aromatic only if it contains $4n + 2$ π electrons. This is true of compounds B, C, and D, but compound A contains only a $4n$ π system and therefore is not aromatic.

198. (B) The Br adds as Br^+ (followed by H_2O attacking to form the alcohol), and the Markovnikov product forms.

199. (C) The –COOH is a meta-director (eliminating answers A and B). Both –COOH and $–NO_2$ are deactivating.

200. (A) The nitro group is a meta-director, so substitution will occur in the meta position.

201. (A) HBr in the presence of peroxide will add across the double bond in 1-pentene in an anti-Markovnikov fashion to give I as the product.

202. (B) A Lindlar catalyst leads to partial hydrogenation, not complete, so an alkene will form over an alkane. The other compounds should not form.

203. (A) The reaction of meta-chloroperoxybenzoic acid (mCPBA) with 4-methylcyclohexene gives an anti-addition, to give an enantiomeric pair of trans diols.

204. (C) Permanganate will react with the cyclohexene to form a diol through syn-addition.

205. (A) A Markovnikov hydration begins with the formation of the most stable carbonium ion. A tertiary carbonium ion will be more stable than a secondary or a primary one.

206. (C) These compounds are nonsuperimposable mirror images of each other. They are enantiomers.

207. (A) What you have here is a racemic mixture, equal amounts of two enantiomers, rotating plane-polarized light in opposite directions and in the same amount. Therefore, the specific rotation is 0°.

208. (D) The addition of HBr to an alkene is a two-step process with the formation of a carbocation. It is not a free radical reaction, and the addition is a Markovnikov addition.

209. (D) The addition reaction of a strong acid to an alkene in the presence of peroxides is a two-step process with the formation of a carbocation intermediate. The first step is the initiation step with the formation of a free radical. Because of this free radical mechanism, the product is anti-Markovnikov.

210. (A) The aromatic system is very stable and acts as a poor nucleophile in electrophilic substitution reactions.

211. (C) Catalysts allow reactions to proceed at faster rates than the uncatalyzed reaction. This is the case here. In general, the hydration will occur without the acid, but much more slowly. Remember, catalysts lower the activation energy. The heat of reaction is a thermodynamic argument, which, in general, does not apply to kinetics.

212. (C) The structure of TNT is a toluene ring with three nitro groups ($-NO_2$) attached. All the groups are the same, so that eliminates answers B and D. The N=O bond is a double bond (eliminating answer A) that involves sp^2 hybridization.

213. (B) In order to end up with the specified product, one must add a hydrogen atom and a bromine atom across the double bond. The bromine is ending up on the more substituted carbon. This is a Markovnikov addition. HBr will accomplish this.

214. (A) A nitro group attached to an aromatic ring tends to withdraw electron density from the ring, deactivating it. In order to add second and third nitro groups, you must increase the temperature to give the species more kinetic energy to overcome the activation energy.

215. (A) Letting the reactant be the solvent eliminates competition from other substances. All the other choices would compete with the chloride.

216. (D) This compound has the strongest electron-withdrawing group adjacent to the double bond. The presence of electron-withdrawing groups increases the strength of the dienophile.

217. (C) Loss of a chloride ion leaves a carbocation that is stabilized by inductive effects; this is then followed by meta attack.

218. (B) Syn addition will occur under these anti-Markovnikov reaction conditions.

219. (A) Reaction with the sulfuric acid leads to the generation of the carbonium ion, which will rearrange to a more stable carbocation.

220. (C) All are o,p-directors. The larger the group, the greater the steric hindrance at the ortho position; this leads to more para product.

221. (D) Ozonolysis cleaves the double bonds, which separates the top of the molecule from the bottom. Since the two halves are identical, there is only one product.

222. (A) This combination of reactants is a typical Markovnikov situation. The chlorine adds to the double bond, and the hydrogen can add either syn or anti to the carbon atom, which already has the greater number of hydrogen atoms.

223. (D) Relative to benzene (answer A), the methoxy group (answer D) is activating (faster reaction), while the aldehyde (answer B) and the acid (answer C) are deactivating.

224. (A) Resonance induced by electron-withdrawing groups leads to the withdrawal of electron density from the ring, which in turn, leads to the ring being electron poor and less of a target to electrophiles. Lowering the electron density leads to the system becoming a target for nucleophiles.

225. (C) The other compounds will produce the following: compound A = primary alcohol, compound B = an acid-base reaction to yield a salt, and compound D = tertiary alcohol.

226. (D) Looking at the rate law, it is apparent that the reaction is second order: first order with respect to the alkene and first order with respect to the hydrogen halide. Answer C is correct about the rate-determining step. The rate law does not indicate anything about the number of steps in the mechanism.

227. (A) In aromatic substitution reactions, the aromatic ring acts as a nucleophile due to the presence of the double bonds. A dienophile has an electron-withdrawing group conjugated to the alkene. This is not the case with the aromatic ring.

228. (C) Conformers refer to rotation around a single bond, enantiomers must have a chiral center, and geometric isomers refer to orientation around a double bond or ring. The 2-nitrotoluene and 4-nitrotoluene are constitutional (structural) isomers.

229. (B) The acid-catalyzed addition of water produced an alcohol. It starts with initial protonation of the double bonds and has a carbocation intermediate, with a Markovnikov product. It is only anti-Markovnikov if diborane/peroxide is used.

230. (D) The products do form a racemic mixture since they are enantiomers. The reaction will be second order: first order in HBr and first order in 1-butene. There is no carbocation intermediate formed. However, it is not possible to separate the enantiomers by fractional distillation, since they will have the exact same boiling point. Only some stereoselective means of separation may be used.

231. (A) Ozonolysis will cleave all the double bonds, yielding four pieces. However, three molecules (formaldehyde) are the same, so only two products will form.

232. (B) The HBr addition to 1-pentene will yield the Markovnikov product, II.

233. (D) In this reaction one Br attacks one end of the C=C, and then the other Br attacks. The attack can be from either side to give both enantiomers. Therefore, a racemic mixture will result.

234. (D) This is a hydrogenation (deuterium, D_2, in this case) reaction, and these reactions produce a syn-addition product.

235. (B) Hydrogenation using Na/ammonia produces a trans-alkene from an alkyne.

236. (A) This is a Friedel-Crafts alkylation to add an ethyl group. The isopropyl group is an o,p-director, but steric hindrance at the ortho position means that the para product will predominate.

237. (A) This is a Diels-Alder reaction involving a conjugated diene and a dienophile. The triple bond becomes a double bond, and the two double bonds lead to one double bond between their original positions. The final product should have two carbon-carbon double bonds.

238. (B) The reaction is S_N2, the rate law is rate = k [electrophile] [nucleophile]. Halving the volume doubles both concentrations, so the rate increases by 2^2.

239. (D) This reaction will involve the formation of a carbonium ion, and a tertiary carbonium ion will be the most stable.

240. (C) Hydration of an alkene will produce regioisomers (sometimes called positional or structural isomers).

241. (D) This is a nitration reaction. The carboxylic acid group is a deactivating metadirector, so the nitro group will add in the meta position.

242. (A) The zinc amalgam acts as a reducing agent.

Chapter 5: Nucleophilic and Cyclo Addition Reactions

243. (C) The carbonyl reacts with one alcohol group to give a hemiacetal, which goes on to react with the second alcohol group to yield the acetal.

244. (C) Tautomerism is the process by which an aldehyde or ketone is in equilibrium with its enol form.

245. (A) This reaction forms an imine (answer A). The other product is water (2 H from N and an O from the carbonyl).

246. (B) This is the formation of a cyclic acetal. Under acidic conditions, carbonyls and alcohols react to form acetals.

247. (C) The Grignard reagent behaves as a nucleophile when added to a carbonyl group (attacking the carbonyl carbon), giving a magnesium alkoxide, which the acid converts to the alcohol.

248. (A) This is a saponification reaction (hydrolysis of an ester under basic conditions); the other product is an alcohol (methanol).

249. (B) This reaction forms an ester through the reaction of an acid chloride and an alcohol. The alcohol is a nucleophile attacking the carbonyl carbon, followed by loss of chloride and H$^+$.

250. (D) Only answer D has the methyl group in the right position on the chain to yield the carboxylic acid with the methyl group in the 3-position and a five-carbon chain. The acid side is the carbonyl side of the carbonyl group, while the other side is the alcohol side.

251. (A) Only primary alcohols will oxidize in this fashion to carboxylic acids. Secondary alcohols (answer B) give ketones, and tertiary alcohols (answer C) and phenols do not react. Phenols (answer D) do not react. Only answer A is a primary alcohol.

252. (B) The reduction with lithium aluminum hydride will produce an alcohol. Then reaction with an organic acid will yield the ester B.

253. (B) The nitro group withdraws electron density by an inductive effect, especially in the ortho position, weakening the O-H bond and making it a stronger acid. There is also resonance stabilization of the conjugate base, which also contributes to making the acid stronger.

254. (D) The bromide is a better leaving group, making the compound more reactive.

255. (A) A hemiacetal has the general formula of RC(OR')(OH). Structure A fits this general formula.

256. (B) The halide ions are good leaving groups, allowing them to easily undergo addition-elimination reactions.

257. (D) Hemiacetal formation through the reaction of an alcohol with an aldehyde normally follows second-order kinetics: first order in both the alcohol and aldehyde.

258. (B) These conditions are typical for an aldol condensation. Compound B is an aldol condensation product.

259. (A) The reaction of an enolate anion of a carbonyl compound with another carbonyl compound is the general form of a reaction called an aldol condensation.

260. (D) The presence of the highly electronegative fluorine withdraws electron density from the carbonyl group by inductive effects, weakening the O-H bond, allowing it to leave easier and making it a stronger acid. The closer the fluorine is, the greater the inductive effect and the stronger the acid. Therefore, IV, in which the fluorine is on the same carbon that the carbonyl is attached to, should be the strongest acid, followed by III (fluorine attached to adjacent carbon), then I (fluorine attached two carbons away), and finally II, the weakest acid since there are no fluorine atoms in the structure.

261. (D) An acetal results from the reaction of an alcohol with either an aldehyde or a ketone (in the presence of acid).

262. (D) The hydrogen atoms on the central carbon atom are adjacent to two carbonyl groups, which induce an increased δ+ on the central hydrogen atoms. Loss of one of the central hydrogen atoms (as H⁺) leads to a resonance-stabilized anion. Adjacent to a carbonyl (B) is greater than answer A and less than answer C. Adjacent to a carbonyl and an alcohol is greater than answer B but less than answer D.

263. (A) The conditions are typical aldol condensation conditions. Aldehyde plus acid will lead to an aldol condensation to form a hydroxy aldehyde.

264. (C) It is possible to break an amide by either acid- or base-catalyzed hydrolysis. Acid hydrolysis yields the ammonium ion, and the carboxylic acid and base hydrolysis yields the amine and the carboxylate ion.

265. (A) The strong base removes an H⁺ from the carbon adjacent to the carbonyl to produce an enolate ion. The enolate ion reacts with more aldehyde to form an alkoxide ion, which interacts with water to yield an aldol.

266. (D) The reaction of an acid anhydride with an alcohol is a common procedure for producing an ester.

267. (D) There must be an α-hydrogen present. Hydrogen adjacent to a carbonyl (an α-hydrogen) is acidic. Answer D has no α-hydrogen atoms; therefore, it is not acidic and it will not react with a base.

268. (A) The strong base removes an H⁺ from the carbon adjacent to the carbonyl to produce an enolate ion. The enolate ion reacts with more aldehyde to form an alkoxide ion, which interacts with water to yield an aldol.

269. (C) The conversion of a carbonyl to an alcohol is a reduction. Both answers A and C contain strong reducing agents. Sodium borohydride (answer A), while a very strong reducing agent, is not strong enough to reduce the carbonyl. Lithium aluminum hydride (answer C) is sufficiently strong to reduce the carbonyl.

270. (D) The electron-withdrawing oxygen atoms weaken the carbon-carbon bond holding the acid group to the remainder of the compound. The closer the carbonyl is to the acid, the weaker the bond and the stronger the acid. A weaker bond facilitates the loss of carbon dioxide. Answer D has the acid and carbonyl groups closest to each other.

271. (C) The Grignard reagent attacks the carbonyl group. This is a nucleophilic attack, and it will add an ethyl group to the carbonyl carbon (giving two ethyl groups). The carbonyl group becomes an alcohol.

272. (A) Methoxide is a stronger nucleophile than propoxide since it has few carbon atoms available to stabilize the charge. The more stable propoxide ion is a better leaving group.

273. (B) The acid destroys the acetal, converting the "ether" groups to alcohols and giving a carbonyl.

274. (A) Two functional groups are necessary, one on each end. The two functional groups must be capable of reacting with the amine in the other compound. The acid chloride groups are the only functional groups shown that will readily react with amines. Only answer A has two reactive acid chloride groups.

275. (D) The carbonyl carbon atoms were originally connected by a C=C; therefore, loop the chain around to get the two carbonyl groups together, remove the oxygen atoms, and put a C=C in their place. The product will not have a C=C. The procedure does not yield an alcohol.

276. (A) Aldehydes react with amines to form imines, not amides. The others will yield the amide shown (heating is necessary for benzoic acid).

277. (A) Normally a strong acid will cleave the ether to give first an alcohol and an organic halide, and then the alcohol reacts with the strong acid to become a second molecule of the organic halide. However, in this case, the intermediate "alcohol" is a phenol, which does not react further.

278. (D) The reaction is an acid-base neutralization reaction, which produces the salt shown.

279. (A) The enolate ion is a strong nucleophile, which attacks the carbonyl carbon atom to give the observed product.

280. (B) Dehydration (loss of water) to form an alkene is an elimination reaction.

281. (C) If there is insufficient ammonia, the reaction stops after the acid-base neutralization step to produce the ammonium salt.

282. (A) The conversion of an alcohol to a carbonyl is an oxidation. The only choice that is an oxidizing agent is answer A.

283. (D) The conversion of a carbonyl to an alcohol is a reduction.

284. (B) This is an unfavorable resonance form because of the bad charge distribution. Oxygen is the more electronegative atom; therefore, it is the least likely to stabilize a positive charge, especially when adjacent to a negatively charged carbon.

285. (A) The Grignard reagent plus acid workup converts the carbonyl group to an alcohol. Answer A is an alcohol, answer B is a carbonyl, answer C is a C-H, and answer D is a C=C.

286. (C) Sodium bicarbonate is weakly basic, and it will extract only "strong" acid. The compounds are I = aldehyde, II = alcohol, and III = carboxylic acid. There are too many carbon atoms for the alcohol to exhibit significant solubility in water (or aqueous sodium bicarbonate).

287. (A) Fats are esters, and either acid- or base-catalyzed hydrolysis will break the ester group. Both methods yield the alcohol (glycerol), but acid catalysis yields the carboxylic acid, while base hydrolysis yields the carboxylate ion. The other reactions will not produce a carboxylate ion.

288. (D) Benzyl acetate is an ester. All the reactants listed, except the alcohol, will react with benzyl alcohol to form benzyl acetate. In general, the reactivities are in this order: acid chloride > acid anhydride > acid. Therefore, the acid chloride is the best reactant.

289. (A) The acid-catalyzed reaction between an alcohol and a carboxylic acid is the Fischer esterification and results in the formation of an ester with the elimination of water. The specific reaction here would be: $C_6H_5COOH + HOCH_2CH_3 \rightarrow C_6H_5COOCH_2CH_3 + H_2O$.

290. (C) The reaction between chloroacetic acid and ammonia is an acid-base reaction. There will be a proton donated from the acid to the ammonia (Lewis base) with the formation of an ionic compound, ammonium chloroacetate.

291. (A) You started off with three double bonds (three π bonds) and ended up with one double bond (one π bond). This means that you have lost two π bonds, and those have been converted to two single bonds (two σ bonds).

292. (B) Saponification is base hydrolysis. The base hydrolysis of an ester gives a carboxylate ion (I) and an alcohol (III).

293. (A) The acidity of the compound is related to the strength of the C-H bond and the stability of the anion produced. The hydrogen in position 4 is a hydrogen atom in the α position to each of two carbonyl groups. The two carbonyl groups increase the polarity of the C-H bond, which makes it more acidic. The loss of this H leads to resonance stabilization with each of the carbonyl groups. Therefore, this hydrogen should be most easily lost (most acidic).

294. (D) Compound I has two electron-withdrawing nitro groups, which can delocalize the charge on the conjugate base. III is stronger than II because there is resonance stabilization of the conjugate base of the ortho form.

295. (C) An acetal has $R_2C(OR)_2$, like structure III, while a hemiacetal has $R_2C(OR)$ (OH), like structure I. Structure II is neither an acetal nor a hemiacetal.

296. (D) The molar mass of acetic acid, CH_3COOH, is 60 g/mole. The experimental determination of the molar mass is twice the expected value, 120 g/mole. This is because that acetic acid exists in the vapor phase as a dimer, which the two molecules held together by strong hydrogen bonds.

297. (A) The electron density is localized on the carbonyl oxygen, as shown in the following:

298. (D) The chloride ion is the leaving group. The water has an unpaired electron pair, making it the nucleophile, and the benzoyl chloride is seeking the electron pair, making it the electrophile.

299. (C) Treating an aldehyde with a hot base (forming a nucleophilic enolate ion) gives an aldol reaction followed by dehydration, loss of a water molecule.

300. (D) This is a Claisen condensation, in which an ester enolate attacks a carbonyl group, generating a new carbon-to-carbon bond.

301. (D) Terminal alkynes are acidic, and the Grignard is basic. The other product is propane.

302. (A) In general, the reactivities are in this order: acid chloride > acid anhydride > ester > ether.

303. (C) Pyridinium chlorochromate (PCC) is a mild oxidizing agent that will partially oxidize a primary alcohol to an aldehyde, instead of a complete oxidation to a carboxylic acid. Compound C is the only aldehyde.

304. (A) Hydrogen atoms on the carbon atom adjacent to a carbonyl group are acidic. Structure II has no carbonyl group, so it would not function as an acid at all. In I, there is a carbonyl group, but in III, the hydrogen atoms on the central carbon are adjacent to two carbonyl groups, making it the strongest acid.

Chapter 6: Lab Technique and Spectroscopy

305. (B) Sodium hydroxide would convert the boric acid to water-soluble borate ion, which ends in the aqueous layer. The organic compounds would probably be in the ether layer.

306. (A) The compound is symmetric, so it is only necessary to consider one side. Starting from the left and counting to (and including) the carbonyl carbon, there are four different carbon atoms.

307. (D) There are five different chemical environments for the carbon atoms: the methyl carbons, the ring carbon between the methyl substituents, the carbons the methyl groups are attached to, the carbons that are ortho to the methyl substituents, and the carbon that is meta to the methyl groups.

308. (A) Due to the selectivity of bromine, the predominant product has the bromine atom attached to the tertiary carbon atom. In this product, all of the hydrogen atoms are in equivalent methyl groups with no hydrogen atoms on the adjacent carbon atom (where the bromine is). Therefore, there would be only one signal.

309. (A) There are no hydrogen atoms on the carbon that the methyl or methylene groups are attached to; therefore, the peaks would be singlets because there is no coupling. The alcohol group gives another singlet. All other compounds have some hydrogen atoms on two adjacent carbon atoms; this leads to coupling.

310. (D) Aqueous sodium bicarbonate will extract the carboxylic acids (all the compounds). In any case, all of the chemical species can hydrogen bond to water and therefore will be soluble in the aqueous layer.

311. (B) Diisopropyl ether would not have a C=C stretch. The absence of this in the IR spectrum would eliminate propene as a possible product.

312. (A) Sodium bicarbonate will extract acids like the carboxylic acid (II); however, phenols are too weak to react. Compounds II and IV can hydrogen bond strongly to water, and thus they would be in the aqueous layer.

313. (A) Compound I has four kinds of hydrogen that have different chemical environments (four signals), II has two types of hydrogen atoms (two signals), III also has two types of hydrogen atoms (two signals), and IV has only one type of hydrogen (one signal).

314. (C) The reaction produces carbonyls (1700 cm^{-1}), not alcohols (3300 cm^{-1} and 1300 cm^{-1}) or ethers (1250 cm^{-1}).

315. (A) The difference in boiling points can be attributed to the difference in the intermolecular forces. In 1-chloro-2-methoxyethane, the strongest intermolecular force would be the dipole-dipole attraction, which is weaker than hydrogen bonds. In the case of 1-chloro-2-propanol, an alcohol, there would be hydrogen bonding, a strong intermolecular force, which would make its boiling point higher.

316. (D) Amines (answer A) show absorption in the 3250–3500 range, alkynes (answer B) 2100–2260 and 3260–3600, alcohols (answer C) 3200–3650, and aldehydes 1690–1,750 (carbonyl). The correct answer is D, an aldehyde.

317. (C) Extraction, chromatography, and distillation are all separation techniques, while IR spectroscopy is a technique used to determine the structure of a compound.

318. (B) NMR is not a separation technique; thin layer chromatography can be used for identification, but not for an actual separation (especially if large quantities are present); and extraction would involve finding a solvent that one of the compounds is insoluble in and then removing the solvent at the end. There should be a significant difference in the boiling points of these two compounds since the alcohol can hydrogen bond to other alcohol molecules and the other compound cannot. Therefore, distillation should be the simplest method for separating a mixture of the two.

319. (A) An appropriate chemical separation will yield the separate component enantiomers. Separation techniques should not produce another racemic mixture, and no diastereomers will form. There is no loss of optical activity during chemical separation, because nothing is changing the chiral centers.

320. (C) The separation of enantiomers is called resolution. The other three answers are general laboratory techniques for separation or purification that will not separate enantiomers.

321. (B) Mass spec will confirm the chlorination, but would give no structural information in this case. IR and UV-Vis would again confirm the chlorination, but cannot easily differentiate between the possible structures. NMR, on the other hand, would be able to discern the differences in the structures.

322. (A) Filtration does not work well with many mixtures; there must be a solid involved. IR is not used for separating mixtures, but for structure determination. Ultracentrifugation only works if there is a very large difference in molecular weights. Chromatography can be used for separating mixtures in many cases.

323. (D) Because of the slight differences in the chemical environment of the nitro groups in the two compounds, NMR would be the best way to distinguish between the compounds.

324. (C) The toluene is nonpolar, and it does not interact with the silica gel, which is polar. The nitrotoluene, however, is polar, and it will interact with the silica gel, slowing it down with respect to toluene.

325. (A) In the 1,3,5-trinitrobenzene, there are two different types of carbon atoms: those with nitro groups attached (all identical) and those with hydrogen atoms attached (all identical). Therefore, you should observe two peaks in the ^{13}C NMR spectrum.

326. (D) The best way would be through NMR spectroscopy. The chemical environments are greatly different in these two compounds, so NMR could easily pick them out. Mass spectroscopy would not be very useful in this case, thin layer chromatography would also not be very useful because of the lack of difference in the polarity of the molecules, and the UV-Vis would yield a complex spectra.

327. (B) The compound is symmetric, so it is only necessary to consider one side. Starting from the left and counting to the center (not including the carbonyl carbon since it has no hydrogen attached), there are three different carbon atoms giving three different types of hydrogen atoms.

328. (A) Lithium aluminum hydride converts carbonyl groups to alcohols. Therefore, the increase by four hydrogen atoms indicates that the two carbonyl groups underwent reduction. Heating an alcohol with sulfuric acid leads to dehydration. There are two alcohol groups; therefore, there are two possible dehydrations. Each dehydration produces an alkene with the loss of an H_2O.

329. (C) This is an OH stretch. The only compound choice with an OH group is the alcohol.

330. (D) The three methoxy groups each contain three hydrogen atoms with no other hydrogen atoms nearby to couple with them. Compound A has only two methyl groups. In compounds B and C, at least one methyl group can couple with hydrogen atoms on the adjacent carbon atom.

331. (A) Hydrogen bonding (1-pentanol) is a stronger intermolecular force than the dipole-dipole force in 1-bromopentane. The higher molecular weight leads to a slight increase, and polymerization is not an option.

332. (A) Ultraviolet-visible spectroscopy is also known as electronic spectroscopy. Infrared spectroscopy deals with vibrating bonds. Mass spectroscopy, as the name implies, deals with the mass. NMR spectroscopy looks at nuclei.

333. (D) The IR gives the carbonyl, the NMR and Tollens' test eliminate an aldehyde, leaving only a methyl ketone to generate the iodoform.

334. (A) TLC plates are polar, and polar materials (sulfonic acids) travel less than nonpolar materials (toluene).

335. (A) Sodium bicarbonate reacts with acids to produce water-soluble borates. The alcohol and ester are more soluble in ether.

336. (D) There are 14 different types of carbon atoms (all the carbon atoms are different).

337. (B) The splitting of proton NMR signals depends upon the number of hydrogen atoms on the adjacent carbon atoms. If there are n hydrogen atoms, then the adjacent hydrogen atoms are split into $n + 1$ peaks. A triplet (three peaks) is due to two hydrogen atoms on the adjacent carbon atom.

338. (C) A band in this region is a carbonyl (eliminating answer D). Answers A and B both have two oxygen atoms; however, there is only one oxygen atom in the formula, which eliminates answers A and B.

339. (B) Deshielding shifts the signal to higher ppm values.

340. (C) The procedure will convert a carbonyl (ketone) to an alcohol (one new signal) and add a hydrogen atom to the carbon atom formally part of the carbonyl (a second new signal).

341. (A) Alcohols have a strong absorption in the 3200–3550 cm^{-1} region. All the others contain a carbonyl group (1715 cm^{-1}).

342. (D) Distillation and extraction will work for large amounts of material, but the other two choices will not. Extraction with aqueous base requires an acid, but none is present. Only distillation remains.

343. (A) Water removes unreacted ammonium formate. Acid converts the amine to water-soluble ammonium ion (leaving the carbonyl compound unreacted and in the organic layer).

344. (A) Base removes hydrogen ions, leaving an overall negative charge, while acid adds hydrogen ions, leaving an overall positive charge. Positive ions move toward the negative plate, and negative ions move toward the positive plate.

345. (B) The less polar compound will migrate farther (larger value) than the more polar compound. Molecular mass is much less important to TLC.

346. (D) The change in position indicates a change in the carbonyl region of the compound. HCl hydrolysis will convert an ester into a carboxylic acid with retention of a carbonyl peak. The ether has no carbonyl peak. Neither a ketone nor a carboxylic acid will change under these conditions.

347. (A) This is the iodoform test for a methyl ketone.

348. (D) Lithium aluminum hydride converts carbonyl groups to alcohols. Therefore, the increase by four hydrogen atoms indicates that the two carbonyl groups underwent reduction. No C=C underwent reduction. There is one degree of unsaturation that could be a double bond or a ring. The question asked for the maximum number of rings; therefore, there is one ring.

349. (A) Homolytic cleavage produces two free radicals. This is the initiation step in a free radical mechanism.

350. (D) There are two types of carbons present here: six secondary and two tertiary. All of the secondary carbon atoms are equivalent as are the tertiary carbons. Therefore, the NMR spectra should yield two peaks.

351. (C) Spin-spin coupling occurs when hydrogen atoms on one atom interact magnetically with different hydrogen atoms on an adjacent atom. In compounds A and D, there are no hydrogen atoms on adjacent atoms. In compound B, all the hydrogen atoms are equivalent, so there will be no coupling. In compound C, there are hydrogen atoms on adjacent carbon atoms, so coupling should take place.

352. (B) Amines (answer D) show absorption in the 3250–3500 range; alcohols (answer C), 3200–3650; aldehydes (answer A), 1690–1750; and alkynes (answer B), 2100–2,260 and 3260–3600. The correct answer is B, an alkyne.

353. (A) Amines are bases; therefore, treatment with a strong acid will protonate the amine, forming a cation (ammonium) and making it water soluble.

354. (B) Isobutane has the formula of $CH(CH_3)_3$. Highly selective bromination produces primarily $CBr(CH_3)_3$. The methyl hydrogen atoms are equivalent, and there are no hydrogen atoms on the adjacent carbon atom to cause splitting.

355. (D) Filtration is out; both are liquids. Extraction is out, with either acid or base; it is difficult to form ions with an alcohol or ether. Fractional distillation will work since the ether is polar with dipole-dipole forces, but the alcohol has a stronger intermolecular hydrogen bond. This will make a significant difference in their boiling points, with the alcohol having the higher.

356. (A) Since there are no H atoms on the adjacent C, there will be no splitting and a singlet will be observed.

357. (D) The formula, C_nH_{2n}, indicates that the compound has either one ring or one double bond. All compounds of more than three carbons with a double bond would show more than one NMR peak. Therefore, the compound must be cyclobutane, since all the hydrogen atoms would have the same chemical environment.

358. (A) In structure I, there are two types of carbons (those attached to an OH group and those not attached), so there would be two ^{13}C NMR signals. In II, there are four types of carbons (four signals). In III, there are four types of carbons (four signals). In IV, all the carbons are equivalent, so there would be only one signal.

359. (C) The reaction shown is the oxidation of a secondary alcohol, which yields a ketone. The absence of the O-H stretch would indicate that all the alcohol had been converted to the ketone.

360. (D) The amine group on III is basic, so extraction with dilute HCl will protonate the amine group, forming a water-soluble ion. The other materials do not react with acid, and they remain in the organic layer.

361. (A) Titration is not a separation technique, eliminating answer D. There would not be enough difference in properties of the products to use solvent extraction. Paper chromatography is only useful for very small amounts of sample. Since there is 100 mL mixture, fractional distillation would be the most logical.

362. (D) IR absorption in the 1700 cm^{-1} is indicative of a C=O bond, which all three have.

363. (C) The 3600 cm^{-1} absorption in the IR spectrum is indicative of an O-H stretch. The base (OH$^-$) would be left behind in the separated water layer.

364. (A) Since there are hydrogen atoms with different chemical environments, ^{1}H NMR spectroscopy would be the best choice in identifying the various products.

365. (B) The aromatic system has three different hydrogen environments; therefore, there will be three resonance signals. (There are no hydrogen atoms on the carbon atoms with methyl groups attached.)

366. (A) The average of the two pK$_a$ values is 5.4 (= pI). At the pI, the overall charge is 0; therefore, the amino acid will not migrate.

Chapter 7: Bioorganic Chemistry

367. (A) The presence of the electron-withdrawing nitro groups makes the aromatic ring very electrophilic. The amine end is a stronger nucleophile than the acid end. The stronger nucleophile attacks the electrophile.

368. (B) To determine the absolute configuration about a carbon atom, note the lowest priority group and assign priority to the other groups. Beginning with the highest priority group (N), count toward the next highest group and end with the lowest group. Counting to the right (clockwise) is R, and counting to the left (counterclockwise) is S. The configuration about each carbon atom is independent of the configuration around the other carbon atom. Doing this, the counting is counterclockwise or an S configuration.

369. (C) Amino acids are considered to be amphoteric because they can behave as both an acid and a base. They have a carboxylic acid end that can act as a proton donor (acid) and an amine end that can act as a proton acceptor (base).

370. (A) This is a linkage between carbon 1 (left-hand glucose ring) of the α-anomer with the carbon 4 on the other ring.

371. (C) Dipeptides form by linking two amino acids with water being released. This is not the case here since this involves the linking of monosaccharides.

372. (D) There are 6 chiral carbon atoms present in the testosterone. The number of stereoisomers can be calculated by 2^n, where n is the number of chiral carbons. Therefore, $2^6 = 64$.

373. (B) The degree of unsaturation is calculated by adding together the number of rings and the number of π bonds in the molecule. In the case of testosterone there are 4 rings + 2 double bonds (π bonds) = 6.

374. (D) A pH of 7.4 indicates that it is slightly more basic than pure water, which has a pH of 7.0. It also means that the concentration of the hydrogen ion is less than the hydroxide ion concentration, so answer D is the correct answer.

375. (C) Since the leucine is immersed in a solution whose pH is the same as its isoelectric point, it will be in the zwitterion form, which has an overall 0 charge. Therefore, it will be attracted to neither electrode.

376. (A) An aldopentose is a sugar that has five carbons (pent = five C's) and is the aldehyde form (aldo = aldehyde). I and III fit those criteria; II has six carbons (hexose) and IV has no aldehyde present (ketose).

377. (D) If they formed smaller rings, there would be a great deal of strain introduced into the structure because the bond angles would be less than in a tetrahedral arrangement.

378. (C) The tertiary structure of proteins places the polar side chains on the exterior of the proteins where they can interact with nearby molecules, such as water.

379. (B) A nucleoside is formed from a nitrogen base and a five-carbon sugar (no phosphate). It can then react with phosphoric acid to form the phosphate ester. This compound is called a nucleotide.

380. (A) Acid chlorides and acid anhydrides are extremely reactive species. They are far too reactive to exist in complex biological systems.

381. (A) The structure of the micelle is a conglomerate with the carboxylate groups (which are hydrophilic—water loving) on the exterior and the nonpolar hydrocarbon tails (which are hydrophobic—water hating) on the interior. Because of this, the solubility of the conglomerate is increased.

382. (C) Glycine is the only amino acid that does not have a chiral carbon. This is because the α-carbon has two hydrogen atoms attached to it, H_2N-CH_2-COOH.

383. (B) The isoelectric point of alanine is the average of the pK_a values of the amine and carboxylic acid group. The same two groups in ornithine will give about the same average; however, the additional $-NH_2$ significantly increases the value.

384. (A) The ammonia is a nucleophile that attacks the carbonyl carbon atom.

385. (D) In each case, the carboxylic acid group gives one pK_a. There is an additional pK_a value for each $-NH_2$ group.

386. (A) All the rings are "locked." It is necessary for the ring to open (making the aldehyde accessible) for the sugar to be reducing.

387. (D) The anomeric carbon atom in unit A is farthest to the right in the ring. The anomeric carbon atom in unit D is the "top" one (connected to unit B). An acetal is $R_2C(OR)_2$, and a hemiacetal is $R_2C(OR)OH$ (the R groups may or may not be the same).

388. (D) Each ring is one unit of unsaturation, and each double bond is another.

389. (D) Maltose is a disaccharide, but all the subunits are monosaccharides.

390. (B) Unit D is the β-anomer. The anomeric carbon in unit D is 1. The connection of unit D to unit B is to carbon 2 in unit B (numbering from the anomeric carbon 1). This combination is B.

391. (C) The structure of the hexapeptide is gly-ala-ser-gly-ser-pro. The 2,4-dinitrofluorobenzene might react with either end; however, since it is with the gly, it must react with the N-terminal amino acid.

392. (A) The gly is terminal because of the reaction with 2,4-dinitrofluorobenzene; therefore, one of the first two tripeptide fragments must be the N-terminus. There is only one ala residue; therefore, the first and last tripeptide residues must overlap, with the ala being the same in each. These tripeptides now give the sequence gly-ala-ser-gly, so the C-terminal gly must be the gly in the remaining tripeptide. Combining the third tripeptide gives the answer. The dipeptides can be used to check the prediction. All structures follow the convention of listing from N-terminus to C-terminus.

393. (B) Peptide bonds (amide groups) undergo hydrolysis with acids or bases. Hot concentrated is better than room temperature dilute. Acids mimic biological systems (stomach) better than bases.

394. (A) Amino groups are typical organic bases. The others are close to neutral if not neutral.

395. (B) The pH is very basic; therefore, all acidic groups will be deprotonated. Both the carboxylic acid group and the weakly acidic phenol group will be deprotonated.

396. (C) There are four chiral carbon atoms (all but the top and bottom). The top half is the mirror image of the bottom half, which makes this a meso compound.

397. (A) Oxidation will convert a secondary alcohol to a ketone. A monosaccharide with a ketone group is a ketose. There are six carbon atoms (a hexose).

398. (D) Both α and β anomeric forms occur naturally, and both D and L enantiomers can occur.

399. (D) The zwitterion form has a protonated amino group (N^+) and a deprotonated carboxylic acid group (O^-). The overall charge is zero.

400. (C) In Fischer projections of carbohydrates, the key is the highest numbered (closest to the bottom) chiral carbon. If the –OH is on the left, it is L, and if it is on the right, it is D.

401. (A) The amino group is basic, and it will react with the acid. No other group would react (be protonated). Protonation leads to a positive, not zero, charge.

402. (B) The α-carbon (adjacent to the carbonyl) in glycine is not chiral. In all other cases, the α-carbon atom is chiral.

403. (D) Count from the oxygen atom in the ring.

404. (B) At the isoelectric point, the amino acid is in its zwitterionic form and the overall charge is zero (neutral). Decreasing the hydrogen ion concentration (increasing the pH) results in the loss of hydrogen ions (positive). Removing positive leaves negative.

405. (A) The nonpolar (hydrophobic) side chain makes it more likely to be in the nonpolar region. All the others are polar (have S or O).

406. (A) Enantiomers will behave identically in cases B, C, and D. This leaves answer A.

407. (A) An α-amino acid has an amino group and a carboxylic acid group (not present in answers C or D) attached to the same carbon atom (the α-carbon). Answer B is a β-amino acid.

408. (C) The hydrogen atom on the chiral carbon atom will split the signal from the methyl hydrogen atoms into a doublet.

409. (D) Only the ionic forms are stable. These involve a charge at one end or the other or on both ends (the zwitterion).

410. (D) In the zwitterionic form of any amino acid, the amino group is protonated and the carboxylic acid group is deprotonated.

411. (A) The low pH will protonate the molecule, which eliminates answer D. The protonated form has a positive charge, which eliminates answer B. At the pK_a of the acid group, the equilibrium involves both the zwitterion and the protonated form (+1 charge).

412. (C) The pH is above both pK_a's; therefore, both the amino group and the carboxylic acid group are deprotonated to the form shown.

413. (A) Sucrose is a disaccharide composed of a glucose and a fructose subunit. Maltose is a disaccharide composed of two glucose subunits. You need to know the common monosaccharides and disaccharides (do not worry about memorizing obscure carbohydrates).

414. (A) The compounds are nonsuperimposable, non-mirror images of each other (therefore, diastereomers), and the only difference is at the anomeric carbon, making them epimers. They are also anomers of each other since they are epimers that differ only at the anomeric carbon. This results in two molecules that fit all the definitions.

415. (D) To determine the absolute configuration about a carbon atom, note the lowest priority group and assign priority to the other groups. Beginning with the highest priority group, count toward the next highest group and end with the lowest group. Counting to the right (clockwise) is R, and counting to the left (counterclockwise) is S. The configuration about each carbon atom is independent of the configuration around the other carbon atom. The carbon with the two carbons attached is not a stereocenter. For both carbons, you would count to the right (R).

416. (C) The O-P-C is typical of a phosphate ester.

417. (A) Isomerization changes one isomer to another. Isomers have the same formula. If the formula changes, it is not an isomerization.

418. (B) Hexoses (monosaccharides with six carbon atoms) can form rings in two different anomeric forms.

419. (C) Partial hydrogenation of a polyunsaturated fat requires the use of hydrogen gas with a nickel catalyst. The fat must be in excess, otherwise complete hydrogenation will occur.

420. (B) The primary structure of a protein is the sequence of amino acids; the secondary structure involves formation of hydrogen bonds between the protein's peptide bonds; the tertiary structure involves side-chain interactions; and the quaternary structure involves the interaction between two or more polypeptide chains.

421. (D) Hydrogen bonds are not really bonds; they are intermolecular interactions and could not hold the amino acids in a protein molecule together. Those bonds are amide bonds.

422. (B) Hydrogenation of the double bonds leads to straighter-chain molecules. Then the nonpolar chains can undergo increased London dispersion forces between the chains.

423. (A) According to the Henderson-Hasselbalch equation, pH = pK_a + log [base] / [acid]. Therefore, substituting the pH and the pK_a into the equation, you get 3.85 = 3.85 + log [base] / [acid]. The entire log term must equal zero, and the only way that this can be mathematically true is that the ratio of base to acid equals 1 (log 1 = 0).

424. (B) The pI is the average of the two pK_a values unless the side chain is also acidic or basic, which is not the case here. The average of 2.35 and 9.69 is 6.02.

425. (D) It is impossible to determine the sequence of amino acids given the results of the hydrolysis.

426. (A) This is the formation of a disulfide bond by removal of two hydrogen atoms. The oxidation of two sulfhydryl groups results in the formation of a disulfide bond. This is a redox reaction, oxidation-reduction.

427. **(D)** Because the straight-chain form is in equilibrium with the ring structures, as the straight-chained structure reacts, the reaction will shift to the left to produce more by the Le Châtelier principle. Therefore, all of it will eventually react.

428. **(A)** The resonance form would involve shifting the double bonds around the six-membered ring. Any structure that moves atoms is NOT resonance.

429. **(D)** Both nitrogen atoms have a lone pair (not shown). A nitrogen atom with a lone pair and three single bonds is sp^3.

Chapter 8: Final Review

430. **(A)** In the acid-catalyzed hydrolysis of an ester, the products are a carboxylic acid and an alcohol. In the base-catalyzed hydrolysis, you get an alcohol, but instead of the carboxylic acid, you get the carboxylate ion.

431. **(C)** An acid anhydride consists of two carbonyl groups linked by an oxygen atom.

432. **(A)** This is the definition of competitive inhibition.

433. **(D)** The hydrogen from the alcohol adds to the center carbon of the isopropyl group (where the Mg was).

434. **(A)** This is the isotope effect. Heavier isotopes react slower than lighter isotopes. This is very important for hydrogen and less important for heavier atoms.

435. **(C)** Sodium bicarbonate is commonly used to extract carboxylic acids.

436. **(A)** This is an S_N2 situation; therefore, inversion of configuration occurs.

437. **(B)** The reactants will undergo an E1/E2 mechanism with the tertiary alcohol reacting the fastest.

438. **(A)** The polymer is the result of the polymerization of a substituted 1,3-butadiene. Polymerization of 1,3-butadienes leaves a C=C double bond in every repeat unit.

439. **(A)** Alkyllithium compounds may (rarely) act as reducing agents, but they never (in aqueous systems) act as oxidizing agents.

440. **(A)** Bromine reacts with trans-3-hexene to give this product.

441. **(B)** The bicarbonate ion, HCO_3^-, has three oxygen atoms attached to a carbon atom and the hydrogen atom attached to one of the oxygen atoms. All resonance forms MUST follow this connectivity (eliminating answers C and D). In answer A, one of the oxygen atoms and the carbon atom do not have a stable octet of electrons.

442. (A) Always begin by making sure that all forms shown are reasonable (e.g., do they all obey the octet rule), because there are situations on the MCAT where "impossible" structures are present. The best (most stable) resonance form has all atoms with a zero formal charge (I). Resonance forms with the most electronegative atom (O) being negative are next in stability.

443. (A) The presence of an impurity leads to freezing point depression.

444. (C) To be exothermic, the final state must be lower than the start (regardless of what is between). This eliminates answers A and D. The rate-determining step had the largest E_a (greatest "jump" in energy). This is the second step in answer B and the first step in answer C.

445. (A) The activation energy to I is less than the activation energy to III (smaller "jump"). The lower activation energy is more rapid. The lower absolute value (III) is the most stable.

446. (C) This is the "ideal" S_N2 mechanism.

447. (A) A carbon atom with three bonds and no lone pairs is sp^2. The ideal sp^2 bond angle is 120°.

448. (D) The stronger the intermolecular forces, the higher the boiling point. (These are all nearly the same size; therefore, size does not matter.) Answer A is nonpolar, which means there are only weak London dispersion forces (lowest boiling point). All the others can form hydrogen bonds, which increases their boiling points. Hydrogen bonding involving nitrogen atoms is weaker than hydrogen bonds involving oxygen (answer B is less than answer C or D). The carbonyl group adds to the polarity of answer D making it higher than answer B.

449. (C) Cyclohexane is nonpolar; therefore, it will preferentially dissolve nonpolar molecules (answer C) over polar molecules (answers A, B, and D).

450. (A) Alcohols are poor acids, but they are definitely better than amines (answers B and C) or alkanes (answer D).

451. (B) All the carbon atoms are equivalent. Therefore, adding one chlorine atom will always give the same product.

452. (A) Free radical bromination is VERY selective. The bromination of the tertiary carbon atom is strongly preferred.

453. (A) Cells are aqueous systems. Water reacts with acid chlorides and acid anhydrides; therefore, these species will not occur in biological systems.

454. (A) Do not forget the unshown hydrogen atoms. Carbon I has four single bonds (three shown plus one to a hydrogen atom), which makes it sp^3. Carbon II has two single bonds (one to a carbon and one to a hydrogen) and a double bond, which makes it sp^2.

455. (A) The key is resonance stabilization.

456. (B) The attack of the free radical on the alkene initiates the polymerization process.

457. (A) The loss of oxygen from an organic compound is a reduction.

458. (A) The loss of C=C leads to the disappearance of the 1650 cm^{-1}. The formation of the carbonyl leads to the increase of the carbonyl (near 1715 cm^{-1}).

459. (D) In order to coordinate to a metal, the side chain must behave as a Lewis base. To serve as a Lewis base, at least one atom needs to have a lone pair of electrons to donate. In amino acids, the atoms that can behave as Lewis bases are nitrogen, oxygen, and sulfur.

460. (A) Assigning formal charges yields a 0 or a –1 for O (overall δ–) and a 0 or +1 for the N's (overall δ+).

461. (A) Begin by focusing on the central atom (the C). This atom has two single bonds and one double bond. This combination makes it sp^2 hybridized with a trigonal planar geometry.

462. (A) The reaction of nitric acid with sulfuric acid produces the strong electrophile NO_2^+.

463. (A) The methyl group is an ortho/para director; therefore, these isomers should result.

464. (A) Intermolecular forces affect melting points, while intramolecular forces do not. Both ortho- and meta-nitrobenzoic acids are polar molecules with no intermolecular hydrogen bonds.

465. (C) An ideal mixture should have the average of the two substances.

466. (A) In the benzene ring (initial) all carbon atoms are sp^2 hybridized. The attack changes one of the carbon atoms to four bonds and sp^3 (intermediate). The loss of a hydrogen atom from the sp^3 hybridized carbon atom gives an aromatic ring with sp^2 hybridized carbon atoms (final).

467. (A) The one with an odd number of electrons is the free radical.

468. (A) The lone electron must be in the unhybridized p-orbital.

469. (C) The pH is above 2.1 and 3.9; therefore, these groups will be deprotonated. The pH is below 9.8; therefore, the amino group remains protonated.

470. (D) Amphoteric substances can behave as either an acid or a base. The carboxylic acid is the acid part, and the amine is the base part.

471. (B) Strong hydrogen bonds hold the two molecules together. All other interactions shown are weaker.

472. (A) The electron-withdrawing carboxylic acid group makes the acid slightly stronger than the alkyl groups, which are nearly identical.

473. (D) All the rings are "locked," so mutarotation cannot occur.

474. (A) In order to form a condensation polymer, two functional groups are necessary (one at each end). Answer A has only one functional group.

475. (A) The most stable structure would be the one in which both bulky side chains are in the equatorial positions.

476. (D) The side chain of asparagine is an amide (which can undergo hydrolysis); all the other side chains are hydrocarbons.

477. (A) An amine will react with an acid to form an amide. A polymer linked by amide groups is a polyamide.

478. (C) The free radical intermediate is planar; therefore, attack may occur from either side with equal probability. From one side the (R) enantiomer forms, and the (S) enantiomer forms from the other side.

479. (D) The molecule is symmetrical; therefore, a Cl on either end is the same compound. The unique positions (giving different compounds) are any of the methyl groups, the center carbon, and the tertiary carbon atoms (each with two methyl groups attached).

480. (A) All the carbon atoms in the ring are chiral, because each has four different groups attached.

481. (D) All double bonds contain a π bond, which gives three π bonds. All single bonds and double bonds have a σ bond. Do not overlook the hydrogen atoms, which do not appear in the figure.

482. (C) The ring gives one, and each double bond gives another.

483. (A) No carbon atoms have four different groups attached.

484. (A) Focus on the differences (sulfonic acids are VERY strong, which eliminates answer C). Phenols are weaker than carboxylic acids, which eliminates answers B and D. This leaves answer A.

485. (D) The largest groups (the methyl groups) are a maximum distance apart, and the remaining groups (H) are also not close. This is the most stable of the three staggered conformations.

486. (B) There are four different types of carbon atoms, which gives four isomers. Addition at carbon 2 or 3 (counting from the methyl carbon) can add either cis or trans relative to the methyl group to give two additional isomers.

487. (D) Free radical stability is in the following order: 3° > 2° > 1°. Answer A is primary, answers B and C are secondary, and answer D is a tertiary (the most stable).

488. (A) It is more difficult to sulfonate benzoic acid than toluene, because the carboxylic acid group is deactivating whereas the alkyl group is activating.

489. (C) Ammonia is a weak base and water is amphoteric. Br is a much larger atom than Cl, so the bond to the hydrogen is weaker in HBr, making it a stronger acid.

490. (D) The balanced reaction for 1 mole of octane is C_8H_{18} + 25/2 O_2 → 8 CO_2 + 9 H_2O.

491. (A) The formula of methylpropane is $CH(CH_3)_3$. There are only two different sites for monochlorination to take place: on one of the methyl groups, or replacing the hydrogen on the tertiary carbon. Therefore, only two products are possible.

492. (C) The reaction between ethyl iodide and hydroxide ion is an E2 elimination to form ethane. This reaction is second order: first order in both ethyl iodide and hydroxide. Tripling both concentrations causes the rate to increase 9-fold, 3 × 3 = 9.

493. (A) BH_3 has a vacant orbital that can accept an electron pair for coordinate covalent bonding. This makes it a Lewis acid.

494. (C) For polymerization there needs to be at least two functional groups or at least one double bond. This is true of all the compounds except the 1-propanol, C.

495. (A) The methyl anion would be the strongest base since it has a pair of unshared electrons on the carbon that can form a coordinate covalent bond with a Lewis acid. The other choices have the electron pair located on a very electronegative element, oxygen or nitrogen, which would tend to attract the electron pair, making it a weaker acid.

496. (D) Hydrogen bonding occurs when a hydrogen atom on one molecule is attached to a highly electronegative element (O, N, or F) and is attracted to an O, N, or F on another molecule.

497. (B) The left carbon atoms on each compound are achiral, and the right C's are simply rotated. There is free rotation around the carbon-carbon single bond. The compounds are the same.

498. (A) Fluorine is more electronegative than chlorine. The fluorine atoms draw electron density away from the O-H bond by inductive effects. The reduced electron density weakens the bond, making it easier for the hydrogen to leave (stronger acid).

499. (B) The left-hand form can only act as an acid; the right-hand form can only act as a base; the zwitterion form can act as either an acid or a base.

500. (B) With HBr and peroxide, the major product will be an anti-Markovnikov addition, as is shown in answer B. Answer A is the free radical product, answer C is the Markovnikov product, and answer D looks nice.

One more. (D) In the first step you are down to 90%; in the second step you are at 30% of the 90% = 27%; in the third step you end up with 70% of the 27% = 18.9%, or about 20% to one significant figure.